APPALACHIAN HERITAGE

VOL. 46, NO. 3
SUMMER 2018

ESTABLISHED IN 1973

PUBLISHED QUARTERLY
by Berea College
CPO 2166
205 N. Main Street
Berea, KY, 40404

www.appalachianheritage.net

 Periodicals postage paid at Berea, Kentucky, and at additional mailing offices. ISSN# 03632318.

Electronic submissions only at www.appalachianheritage.net

Distributed by the University of North Carolina Press. Basic subscription price: $30/year for individuals, $60/year for institutions. For subscription requests and inquiries, visit the magazine's website, email uncpress_journals@unc.edu, or call 919.962.4201.

CONTENTS

INTERVIEW

CRAFT ESSAY

BOOK REVIEW

COVER PHOTOGRAPH

Josh Ness, *Bottle Rocket*

EDITOR'S NOTE

JASON HOWARD

Don't get above your raising. It's a saying with which many, if not most, Appalachians are familiar. I have heard the phrase all my life, particularly from my family and many in my community when I left southeastern Kentucky at eighteen for an internship on Capitol Hill and subsequently to attend university in Washington, D.C. I often considered that admonition as I explored the city, discovering and learning neighborhoods including Dupont Circle and Woodley Park, turning it over and over again in my mind.

On one hand, I appreciated the reminder and its affirmation. *Always remember where you come from. Don't forget your roots.* But I also recognized the other side to this maxim, the implicit cocked eyebrow and finger-wag it also carried. *We're watching you. Don't become too different. There's only one way to be, and we make the rules.*

I was reminded again of this saying after reading Lois Wolfe's wonderful story "Maxims in Winter," which is featured in this issue and includes a number of lessons handed down from a grandmother to a granddaughter. As I reexamined this quintessential Appalachian maxim, I recognized its presence in Savannah Sipple's moving poem "What We Tell Ourselves," in which the narrator is fighting back against strident gender roles and expectations proscribed by her culture, becoming a stranger to her family and community in the process. The complexities of Appalachia are on full display in this poem, and in other writings featured in this issue.

These include "Surface Level," a lyrical new story from Chris Holbrook, an award-winning master of fiction; "The Tennessee Kid," an essay by renowned critic and essayist Hal Crowther about the great musician Jesse Winchester and excerpted from Crowther's new book *Freedom Fighters and Hell Raisers: A Gallery of Memorable Southerners*; a revelatory conversation between bell hooks and Fenton Johnson about solitude, queerness, and home; poems from acclaimed poets including Jeff Hardin, Susan O'Dell Underwood, and others; and a craft essay about magical realism from Rebecca D. Elswick.

Their voices are diverse, different, proving that there is, in fact, more than one way to be in this region. As such, these writers and many of their characters have broken that

Appalachian rule—they have gotten above their raising, and thankfully so. But they have also maintained a fidelity to its central affirmation, remaining firmly rooted in Appalachian soil. They know where they come from.

Nearly twenty years after I mused about it in the streets of D.C., I continue to have a complicated reaction to this maxim, recognizing both its virtues and drawbacks. My typical response is defiance, to quote Walt Whitman: "I contain multitudes." And so, increasingly, does Appalachia—its land, its people, its literature. ■

SURFACE LEVEL

CHRIS HOLBROOK

It was Cecil Leemaster's favorite time on the lake. He'd make his first excursion a few days after Thanksgiving, cruising his bass boat along the resurrected creek channel, following the route of old Highway 7. The late fall drawdown of Cedar Lake by the Corps of Engineers left the twelve mile Burgey's Creek section revealed as patches of broken asphalt, rusted strands of guardrail, and scattered foundation stones of homes and businesses.

That first day out Cecil would navigate Burgey's Creek end to end, from where Voncil Sturgill's hay bottom would now lie, some eighty yards offshore of the Cedar Lake Marina, on up to just below the dam where that one buoy marked the most likely location where Ray Martin's sawmill once stood.

Until the end of winter then, he'd go out as often as the weather would allow, traversing the length of each hollow, from Sawyer's Branch to Poke Berry, from half-a-mile up Right Fork to three miles down Salt Lick and as far over as Haven.

Some days he just drifted along, using his trolling motor only enough to keep free of brush tangles and rocks, staying on the lake the whole of the short winter days with no other company than the few cardinals that flighted among the bare trees, or a grey fox that sometimes strayed after him along the banks, scavenging among the Styrofoam ice chests and bait buckets and other odd rubbish lost or thrown from the pontoon boats that made commotion of the lake each May to August.

He did have spells out there to himself, his mind taking its own wayward courses. He might fall into a daydream of planting corn or mowing hay, the smell of lake water transfiguring into that of upturned earth, cut stalks of ryegrass, a horse in harness. A whole day might return to him like a told story—that time they took and rode bicycles down along Grassy Creek and back along through Hackberry, her in her housedress still; her face shining red and sweaty like a kid's, riding him in rings and laughing at his wobbling clumsiness, at the undone strap of his high-backs, at the loose laces of his brogans flapping the blacktop, snarling the wheel spokes. Or it might be just the barest shade of movement, like the muscles of her calves popping leanly in the tan between her socks and dress hem or the skin of her eyelid caught in some spasm of unspoken emotion.

She did him like that in memory. Dared him. *Where's your pencils at? Where's your paper pad?* He had used to try. He had caught her exactly hundreds of times. In graphite and charcoal. In ink. On every kind and weight of paper. On cotton fiber. On vellum. During one anguished night when freezing rain had him stranded to home, he had drunk a third of a bottle of some clear liquor and, stumbling and crying, raked ashes from the wood stove and on a strip of burlap smudged out a rough, wild sketch that bore her no likeness whatsoever. He had burned it before daylight.

Once and again he might venture onto the sand bars afoot and mark the remains of somebody's homeplace—a pile of chimney stones, the roof beam of a barn, a single algae-blackened cinder-block. He saw more than manufactured function in these remnants. Find a lone sheet of corrugated roofing—off somebody's outhouse, somebody's chicken coop—see it now as a contorted relief of rust bubbles and jagged angles, reds, greys and browns blended in a way that spoke of something not even nameable.

No matter that only he might ever see these transfigurations. That a piece would not rate as a juried crafts-work made it no less a genuine conception of mind and method—*the mind of nature divine, the method of sand and water and amending time.* He cringed at the conceit of his own idle verse. These found pieces he hung at careful angles along the walls of the prefab, metal storage building he used as a workshop. They fought and mingled as he worked to unify them into a form he could not yet imagine.

This current day he nosed into the bank just beneath the Highway 15 overpass, tethering his boat against a blighted willow augured out over the water. The tree's branches trailed down to the water's surface, the thin tendrils stirring in motion with each disturbance of the lake's surface. It was before Christmas still, and the before-noon sun was strong enough to warm his face and make a shimmer on the lake's scant patches of ice.

He had just cracked open a Vienna sausage can and was lifting out the first little pink bite of formed meat when he saw the object fixed in among the willow's exposed roots. When he leaned from the boat to see closer, the sausage dropped into the water with a plop, droplets of jelly floating outward on concentric rings of such exact pattern as to themselves want rendering.

It was a sign, but not only. At its center was an oval shaped plastic inset containing a mercury thermostat. The lettering, almost all, was either muddied over or scoured away. What was traceable, though, was enough, the half-shape of a capital "C," some partial lines of the double "t's," and the colors—vague shadings of red and blue clear enough still despite the overall splotching of rust.

Carter's Little in fulsome cursive bordered the thermostat above. On the half of the sign still sunk in murk read *Liver Pills*. This was long ago when he was a child time beckoning. A sign exactly like this, maybe this sign exactly, had hung on the door of Inez Fugate's general store. He made pause for the memory of it—the big, dark building constructed of rough lumber, one big room to function for everything, like a barn, like a church. And she and him children still, not hardly knowing each other outside of school or Sunday worship or the once and again encounter at Fugate's.

In the summer her hair would be sun-bleached to where it was nearly white, her complexion so dappled with freckles and flecks that she looked all the time dirty-faced and wild. And he would get caught staring and be glowered at fiercely and would back himself against the wall of the store. The sensation of great rough wood splinters and risen nail heads catching at his shirt and skin was a close enough memory to cause him still yet to arch his shoulders and squirm.

Cecil rose onto his knees, meaning to grab for the artifact. Instead he off-balanced himself and fell painfully onto his side against the battered metal tackle box he kept in his boat for no reason but that he always had. He nudged the box from beneath him but didn't sit up yet. The boat was unsettled still, its motion causing Cecil an odd blurriness. Below water, the entanglement of tree roots blurred as with an eddying motion. The sign alone showed clearly to him. He lay in such perfect immediacy to the sign that all he might need do to take it was

The contact of his hand with the chilly water brought his mind clear again; he drew back into himself...

reach out his arm a little, lean out a little, tip the boat a little more, roll himself just a little more to the lake surface and reach in.

The contact of his hand with the chilly water brought his mind clear again; he drew back into himself, rolled onto his back in the boat's center and sat upright. He could not have reached far enough to touch the sign, he saw now. The refraction of light through water and root shadows had made it seem close up, but that was deception.

The willow's exposed roots grew in a tangle below the lake surface. They were tied up in fishing line, bobbers of various sizes and colors hanging within the tangle like decoration. The roots grew matted about the sign, dark coils holding the dear object ensnared as with a will.

He had vague realization of the sun having passed from before him to behind. He lay splayed in the boat through the whole of the short afternoon and made an entertainment of watching the shadow of his raised arm lengthen toward the Carter's Pills sign. It was falling dark, at the point he could no longer see letters or colors or at last even a shape, when Cecil pushed away from the bank, pulled the cord on his trolling motor and nosed around toward the lights of the marina boat ramp. He crossed in darkness so complete above and below that there was no orienting his mind as to his body's location. His neck and the whole of his back tingled. He felt fingers pulling at him in the darkness and twice had to orient the prow of the boat back around to the dock lights. He felt the grief of mortal loss close about his heart and gave up his daylong fight against it.

■ ■ ■

It was a comforting sound—the slow, steady trickle of the carafe filling, the last little whoosh of steam. Lovens poured. Cecil held his mug close beneath his chin to breathe in the steam, the bitter flavor. He blew across the surface of the coffee. He sipped, and shivers ran through him, the coffee the least bit oily in its strength. *It is no better comfort in the world than hot coffee,* Cecil thought. *No better pleasure than a fresh mug early of a cold morning and grey like it is.*

Lovens sat staring at a laptop computer screen, one large hand resting on the keyboard, the other enclosing the mouse. His own mug of coffee sat steaming and untouched next to an unopened container of creamer and two sweetener packets. Lovens was in jacket and tie, his narrow shoulders hunched, the crease between his eyes deepening as he glared at the computer screen, his eyebrows like two grey-brown woolly worms brought into collision.

Cecil stared upward through the steam of his coffee in study of the wall behind Lovens's desk. On the left hand hung a portrait of Jesus Christ—the Good Shepherd kneeling in a field of stone, his face uplifted to heaven, his form haloed in a shaft of holy light—the rendering illuminated by an accent lamp atop the picture's frame. On the right hand was affixed a large gold-colored cross bearing the Redeemer's crucified form, below that a mirror-like plaque etched with The Ten Commandments. On Lovens's desk an oversize white Bible lay in place beside a statuette of praying hands. That these tawdry icons comforted Cecil was not something he would admit even to himself.

"The mortuary business, it's ten percent dealing with the deceased, forty percent dealing with the family and fifty percent dealing with the paperwork," Lovens said. He reached to prepare his coffee. He let out a long sigh, tore the sweetener packets open both together, peeled open the creamer container. Cecil watched, knowing how many times and in what direction Lovens would stir the coffee, knowing which side of the mug he would then tap the stir stick against. He anticipated the first long, over-loud slurp.

It was three years and seven months ago now, on the second day of visitation with her lying in the main parlor, that Cecil had come into the office and sat without asking in the armchair before Lovens's desk. The man had done masterful work; the disfigurement of her last illness had been masked over so well that none could have told her suffering. Her cheeks were plumped out, her color darkened to a likeness almost of health. Her mouth had been set in an expression of something like contentment. Her face overall was so softened in appearance as to argue sleep. *It is asleep she is and not spoiled,* he had thought. *It is rest and not death.*

Lovens did not raise an eyebrow when Cecil came in his office that long ago day. Didn't ask, "What can I do you for?"

Didn't ask anything. He poured them each a cup of coffee and there they sat, and have been sitting regular.

Cecil has always kept cautious talking to Lovens, his remarks kept as close to the weather as possible. He slipped his questions in roundabout, finding their suggestion in the passing talk he and Lovens made over their mugs. "Which percent's the worst?" he asked.

Lovens didn't answer at first. He sipped again from his mug, then once more, holding it before his mouth as he swallowed. His eyes flicked upward suddenly, but Cecil had looked away in time. He'd gotten caught once, leaning forward in expectancy of answer. What he had asked, his question that time, was "How do you do it?"

Something had passed across Lovens's face in that moment, the kindliness darkening with some nature of bile before transmuting to wary solemnity. *Do it?* Lovens could be seen sorting through the varied implications of the question. *Do what?* He'd seemed to strain to make a reply, a light of

He sipped again from his mug, then once more, holding it before his mouth as he swallowed.

slyness and dark knowing in his glowering eyes. As suddenly as he had tensed though, he relaxed, the warm-heartedness coming back flush into his face.

To this present question, he hardly blinked. But just shrugged a little and said, "Paper work. Death certificates, post-mortem reports, wills and pensions; forms for the Social Security Administration, for Veterans Affairs, tracking benefits—just paperwork on paperwork, on and on."

He spread his large hands before the computer in a gesture almost of sanctifying. He was, in his function at least, part-ways clergy. Solace radiated from his form, visible in the way of air shimmering above a warming stove. His voice—deep when speaking, a clear tenor when singing—soothed the grief-stricken. Along with the funeral home calendar he sent out a CD of him singing "Amazing Grace," "Leaning on the Everlasting Arms," "Just a Little Walk with Jesus," a few others.

Behind the funeral home building, and a little off to the side behind where the two vehicles were kept parked—a black Lincoln MKT funeral coach for transport of coffins and a blinding silver Cadillac XTS Limousine for families—sat a long rectangular structure, windowless with white siding to match the main building and dark-colored double doors that in direct sunlight looked like burnished metal.

Cecil had been through those doors in his thinking. He knew what was to be seen. He could close his eyes and conceive the entirety of the space, its furnishings, implements, and materials. Along this long wall, close by the industrial sink, the embalming table with a drain on one end and at the other plastic blocks to keep elevated the deceased's head and torso; in that corner the embalming machine—like an artificial heart with two glass tubes on either side of the front, gauged like thermometers and filled with liquid that rose and fell in display of pressure; in the center of the room, in close proximity of the staging area, an autoclave for sterilizing tools; the trocar and suction pump; a biohazard garbage can and boxes and boxes of surgical gloves placed everywhere in reach.

The question that most grieved Cecil, that he felt he must ask with the devil driving, he did not know even the phrasing of. *Speaking on the funerary arts,* he might have begun, *taking a person. . .taking a person's dead body. . . remains. . .that has been ravaged. . .*

Lovens spread his hands, the fluorescent lights making silver glints within his grey, brown sheep's wool hair. "People don't know," he boomed. Then in a voice nearer to a whisper. "It's a call to serve."

*Who they were. . .what they were. . .*Cecil felt something almost like a migraine spark behind his eyes. There was not pain, but a powerful sensation of humming. He felt he might go blind for a moment. He felt an awful chest-bursting panic that he might begin weeping. *To remake them.*

"For the hour is coming," Lovens said softly, "in which all who are in their graves will hear His voice and come forth."

"A call to serve," Cecil thought, the room a fusion of pulsing colors and unstable shapes.

■ ■ ■

The string tied across the open doorway measured the exact midpoint of the door jamb above and the floor below, cutting Cecil right center of the navel. He stood just shy of contact, as if the length of discolored twine might contain some deadliness not to be chanced—a lethal voltage, a razor sharpness.

The room was as she had kept it. To the far right, before the bricked up fireplace, sat the floral patterned armchair with the doily she had crocheted in the pattern of a fox leaping after grapes; cater-corner to that was the button-tufted settee, its fabric an odd yellowish green the shade of which Cecil had seen nowhere else in the natural or manufactured world; at the left wall was the cedar chest, the old-fashioned iron key still in the lock; alongside that the walnut wardrobe, the brass handles and knobs just barely distinct against the dark wood; the curio cabinet held place in the room's center, next to the framed portrait picture of John Kennedy. It was as she had kept it to the last day.

The string even was of her doing. It had barred his intruding for so many years he could not see back beyond it. This one room she'd kept apart from every other in the house—floor scrubbed, walls washed, mantel piece and furniture polished, breakables carefully dusted—as to await some particular company not ever named. Cecil in his meanness had used to want to ask if it was Jesus she was keeping the room for and would he have to take off his sandals before he entered, shake out his robes.

From where he stood he could imagine, as in a painting, lines marking depth and proportion, tying together each shape and shadow, each space of color, lines progressing to meet and vanish at the center point of JFK's princely head. If he stood long enough and stared long enough, let his vision go blurry, he could see the different aspects of the room disassemble, become just dots of color and geometric shapes.

Sometimes, out of all that undoing, would appear wavering forms that were oftentimes person-like, familiar in motion and dimension. He would turn himself so as only to view them sideways, lest they come too close to real. What he saw askance most often—her bent to her quilting frames, piecing together squares of cloth—caused him more upset than he could bear.

His hallucinations were of the hearing kind as well—scuffing sounds, taps, thuds—nothing not ordinary, nothing not like a person might make just in their everyday habits. *Is it you, old woman?* he'd whispered once, then never again.

The specters that haunted his yard were shadow-natured. They crouched of a nighttime amongst the collected debris of his yard. At his coming, they rose from seeming handiwork amongst fragmented butter churns, amongst moldboards and shares and the ossified leads of horse harness coiled helically in patterns both faultless and wild. *Break up the ground. Lay it off.* Words barely known to memory respoke themselves at his passing. Doubtful silhouettes moved beside him among the floodlit stacks of automobile tires and oil drums and scavenged tractor chassis.

A grasp of sourwood leaves and anvil dust. Drop it by hand. Their voices engendered the sifting of hoe blades through soil, of wind clattering amongst fodder shocks, of a metal bucket chiming within the void of a water well.

It took concentration not to hurry, to try and ignore the prickle of fine hairs rising on his neck and arms. He had not ever learned to whistle and he was as toneless humming as singing. He made conversation though, with his trailing visions, calling agreement to their uncertain statements. *Render out the lard for the old fashioned of it.* Yes, that's right. *The smoke's a goin' to the ground.* Yes, uh huh, yes. *Oh eat this. This is good. Eat it. Eat it. Eat it. Eat it.*

The chain that held the workshop door was old metal, an ancient logging chain eroded from the hillside above his house. The links were wasted thin with rust and it hung more as a kind of charm than for any physical security. He unwound it gently, receiving the powdery rust on this hands in the way of a cleansing before entering the dedicated work space.

The studio lights were of a kind to simulate the sun shining. There were no shadows or even dimness. The convex walls were painted an uncorrupted white, unspattered by any color otherwise, though canvases stretched on wooden frames leaned at precise angles half of the building's length, some vividly hued, others tinted in muddied and somber opposition.

Unsorted piles of medium obstructed the near end of the building—blocks of wood, metal pipes and rods, knotted heaps of electrical wire, flattened cardboard boxes bundled with twine, large blocks of molded Styrofoam, unmatched shoes, doll parts. Out of keeping with the whole lay dozens of disassembled computers with motherboards and CPUs and batteries all exposed in grisly tangles.

He unfolded and set the ten-foot stepladder. At four rungs he had climbed above the level of the craftwork—chairs and stools bottomed with woven birch bark, walking sticks carved as reared up blacksnakes and winding copperheads, dulcimers with heart-shaped sound-holes—these sold steadily at the sidewalk fairs and craft markets, all he cared to make, knickknacks that for all the time spent in crafting cost Cecil not even a fart's worth of remorse to part with.

He could never see his masterwork as a whole. The disarray overwhelmed. Auto-body filler on molding-wire textured the three panels of four-by-eight plywood. The layering was nowhere smooth, though long stretches of it seemed as such in contrast to the severe deeps and rises that made a vista of cratered, rutted background.

The most meaningful of his found objects compiled the overlay. The viewer's eye followed an uncertain vector amongst the blades of garden hoes, the disassembled workings of old car motors, a washboard, a crumpled-up tub, and endless bits and shards of plastic, glass, wood, metal, fabric and stone. He had aimed on one panel to suggest the shimmering star, on another the saw tooth, on a third the drunkard's path, though nothing of what he had rendered came very near a true quilter's pattern.

There was neither equilibrium nor harmony in the composition. To stare and study was to fight drunkenness. He had fallen or nearly fallen from the ladder's fourth rung often enough that he had taken to layering the floor space below with salvaged strips of insulation.

If he held on, though, allowed the blending of surfaces and colors and objects, some suspicion of design would arise in his mind. She was in there, she was in there, amongst the abstraction of recovered trash and junk—not her form, not her features, but her, her.

He would go to work then, no less mindful of the windy murmur of voices at the shed walls—*the sorrel tree blooms angel fingers*—but not so much afraid of them now.

He spent the night reaching tools and artifacts high above his head, his neck locked into a painfully obtuse angle that gave him such a slanted and hazy viewpoint that finally he closed his eyes so as to better realize the vision of his fingertips. In the early dawn he climbed down and turned away. *Look not behind thee, lest thou be consumed.* He thought the verse and murmured it as he made his way, so crippled he could not walk but in a stoop. He came almost to the door before he was compelled to turn.

■ ■ ■

He sat with the newspaper laid open on the kitchen table, his shoulders and neck so rigid still that it pained him just to turn the pages. He was too bleary-eyed actually to read. He stared at the bold print headlines until they lifted from the page and made impression on his half-conscious mind—*Asher Mining Cuts 200 Workers, Judge Disallows Hearings on Status of Disability Checks, Baptist Church Ladies Get Together to Make Peanut Butter Balls.* The news-sheets crackled as he turned them, the sound distorted almost painfully by his powerful tiredness of mind and by the otherwise quiet of the kitchen.

There was a page of nursing home news—*Betty Ann Lee is doing well, Carrie Combs is doing better after hip replacement, Mary Lou Sizemore is doing well, Kathy Ritchie is having good days and bad days.* Cecil swam through the scattered information, not grabbing hold of any one piece. The last items he registered before dropping his head onto his crossed arms were a brief homily among the obituaries—*The Devil is the king of Pride / There is Praise in knowing where your Soul is going / After your Life on earth is Extinguished*—and the Walmart and Food World ads on the back page.

He dreamt vividly. He was with her in the kitchen. They were canning. Glass jars lined the long table and bushel baskets sat stacked to the ceiling, spilling over with peas, corn, beets, green beans. A great pot sat boiling on the stove, the filled jars inside singing as tendrils of steam coiled upward in snakelike shapes. He worked to twist the lid ring onto a jar of bread and butter pickles. His hands would not work right though; the ring and lid kept flying off and juices spilled from the jar. And because he could not put the lid and ring onto the jar, she rose up from the table and left her knife—the blade covered with corn kernels and with shreds of cabbage—and went out the door. For a while then in his dream he ran, chased by some worrying form he could not see and could not get free of. He fought intruders in his house, the pain in his neck and

Glass jars lined the long table and bushel baskets sat stacked to the ceiling, spilling over with peas, corn, beets, green beans.

shoulders transmuting to subconscious injury. At the end he fought sleep, fought it smothering and choking until he came awake enough to know of a certain that he was no longer dying.

He was dry mouthed and chilled with sweat. The newspaper had been creased under his fretful hands and he balled the loose sheets and tore them and threw them toward the sink where they disassembled into shreds and wads and single crimped pages. *Ought to be some better way of saying about Kathie Ritchie's good and bad days,* he thought. *Ought to be some more true words available than "disallowed" and "status."*

He stared for a moment at his hands. They were filthy. Black grime was caked beneath his ragged fingernails and within the lines and creases of his palms. His wedding band was no longer a white gold color. It had been scraped and dulled to a dull shade of pewter. Did hers still keep its polish?

His mind was cottony still as he left the house. He drove with no thought to his actions, the truck maneuvering over the rutted and broken roadway as with its own intent. The road took the same winding course as the creek that ran beside it. Trailer homes stood wherever a wide enough space opened back from the road; houses with barns and sheds took up the larger stretches of flat land on the far side of the creek. Brown and broken corn stalks still stood in many of the garden patches, the fallow dirt otherwise taken by scattered patches of chickweed and deadnettle, here and there the purple blooms of henbit.

Cecil felt a confusion traveling the road. When he came around a turn and passed a wide spot where should have stood a poplar log supporting a basketball rim on a backboard of mismatched lumber pieces, he saw instead a cluster of garbage containers—big, welded-together steel boxes with heavy lids to keep out stray dogs—each with a house number adhered to it and little rows of reflector lights. House numbers, as strange and unfitting as the green street signs that read Possum Trot Lane or Marrowbone Circle.

The drivers of cars he met waved to him, and he waved back, though he was not always certain of the faces; they had the semblance of people he knew, but they appeared to him in an odd, wavering manner—some with the faded aspects of old portrait pictures, others with features that were just varied enough from the familiar that he could not quite say their names.

By the time he was on the lake it was past noontime, and the sunlight, weak as it was through the winter overcast, had burned away the lake water mist. The way through and around the deeps and shallows was as plain as a paved road, and he guided the boat full-out over the glass-smooth surface. He kept his gaze in a straight line above the boat's prow so as not to see directly the shades and specters come to people the sandbars and risen patches of asphalt and eroded house seats.

A wind gust came up, rippling the lake surface, rattling the bare tree branches along the far lakeshore. It made a voice-like sound, a singing. Cecil cut the motor and listened, but the water stilled and the sound faded, leaving no sure impression. He did not move to start the motor right away. The boat moved just slightly, turning on the faint current.

He was ready when she came into view, expecting her. She stood next to a black, crooked little tree on a close-by patch of risen ground. She wore a baseball cap, a dark jacket, and jeans stuffed into high boots that were caked in mud almost to the ankles. He could not comprehend the outfit. It was in no way similar to what she had used to wear. He thought for a second it was some stranger-woman he was seeing. She was in no way ghostly. But then she smiled and raised her hand to wave, and he knew her for sure.

She was speaking. He could hear her voice, but her words broke apart before they came to him. He raised his hand and waved back. "I have put myself to it," he yelled. "I have."

After a while she shrugged her shoulders and slipped her hands into her jacket pockets. She turned and walked across the risen ground and into the lake, her boots sinking hardly at all into the water as she trod shoreward.

He kept waving until she was gone, and then he pulled the cord on his trolling motor and steered back around toward the far bank where the corkscrewed willow stood tangled in fishing line. In a few minutes he was close enough to sling a rope around the willow's trunk and pull the boat into shore and tie up.

The water was murky up against the bank, and at first Cecil could see hardly anything beyond the still flotsam of leaves and pine needles. He rolled up his shirt-sleeve, leaned out of the boat, and dipped in his bare arm. He made a stirring motion, trying both to search with his fingertips and to clear away the floating muck. He began to skim the surface water with his hand, flicking the slimy stuff into the boat. As the blackish matter dispersed, underwater shapes began to show—the coiled roots of the willow, the up thrust butt of a log, a ledge of the cliff face that met the lake on that side.

Finally, the contoured top edge of the Carter's Pills sign appeared. It looked to be settled deeper than he remembered, tilted different. In the slightly rippling water it seemed almost to move, as if being worked by slow force.

Cecil rested. The day was chilly, but not past bearing. He cracked open a can of potted meat and dipped the substance out on the corner of a cracker. The taste was a comfort, salty and tangy. He ate the potted meat and crackers and drank orange pop while he studied. When he finished Cecil tied his trash inside a plastic grocery bag and pinned it beneath the tackle box so it would not be taken by the wind.

He hauled his boat a little closer to shoreward then, until he could touch the cliff face where it rose above the water. Cecil searched the flat of his hand across the worn sandstone and found a crevice he could hold to. He slid out of the boat and slowly into the water until his feet touched the ledge. From there he could reach his free hand down to touch the metal edge of the store sign.

He grasped the lip of the sign and pulled. It kept caught for many long minutes, not in the least budging, then with a vigorous suddenness it came free, leaping from the water like a fish that Cecil had to catch and hold from escaping. He clutched it to his breast until he could calm and breathe easy, then he looked it over. Free of the water it did not gleam or waver. It was just a rectangular shape of painted metal, maybe eighteen inches by nine, so eaten through with rust it barely held together in his hands, the lettering stained and faded, the thermostat at its center brittle and loose-fitting.

He tried to think of his mural with this one piece added but could bring to mind only a confused scattering of shapes and objects. Tiny bits of matter floated in his vision, taking color as they gathered. Fragments of bright blue, of red, and dull yellow clumped together, making first the vibrant forms of clouds and then the semblance of a pieced quilt and then a strange muddied topography that was almost without color. There was nothing added to his understanding. There was nothing made alive.

"Nobody knows your heart." He heard her words then, what she had been trying to call to him across the water, through the wind. "Only you, you have to stand on it."

He crimped the edge of the sign with his fingers, the corroded metal folding like paper. He rapped the sign against the side of the boat. Rust shook loose into the air. The cursive lettering cracked, and fissures ran through what remained of the painted surface. The thermometer fell loose and floated like a fishing bobber, on end in the water. Cecil dropped what remained of the ruined sign into the boat, though he had no more thought for its use. ■

AFTER PLANTING OKRA IN MIDSUMMER

He undresses outside glass doors, throws
down his gloves, shirt, belt and comes
slowly on the rock path to the house.

Make me the bare country—
wind stirring grasses against the hills,
toads slipping the mud, gnats' golden sprawl,
hawk's white stomach
flitting to dead oaks,
all that pulses above
his slender legs, his dark curls.

Make me the earth, held
in his blistered hands, brushed
off after covering the seed, and the seed
on fire inside black loam.
One minute against his skin.

Make me what scrapes on soil,
what floats in sky where he moves
in and out of lacquered woods, returns
from dusk to the edge of the bed
with twigs in his hair.

The smell of sweat on his back
and I become my wild self,
native to this land.
His ribs, a ridgeline

I touch
and open the stars.

NICOLE STOCKBURGER

FULL FLOWER MOON

May 21st

Sun burned scales into my arms
and I saw sweat roll

under your beard as we walked
to the red maple—the one

your family saved when they bought
and cleared the land. Between

kitchen and smokehouse, it fell under
last night's moon, barely leaving space

for breath. You said the task was simple—
toss away broken branches and pile

the truck for firewood. But the day
swarmed with beetles, ivy

pricked our arms, greenbriar
tangled our boots. And after you

dumped logs from the white pickup,
I stayed longer, staring at a green

bud beside the stump, still alive.
I took off my gloves,

gathered the dirt over
roots, and matted them down.

NICOLE STOCKBURGER

THE WRECKER LOT

After the latest town wreck, my mother
would drive us past the wrecker lot
to see the twisted shapes of metal;

bumpers and back ends deranged,
sharp edges glinting; passenger doors
cut away to remove the dying,

the already dead—the bodies, we heard,
sometimes burned beyond recognition.
Evening quiet would come down

from the trees as we sat, motor idling,
on a side street, window rolled down,
radio off, looking through the chain-

link fence. I imagined faces slammed
against dashboards, necks snapped,
doorframes thrust inward, tears,

brain matter, gas tank burst, ribs
mangled, lungs punctured, the slow
beginning of flames, the moment

of recognition.
                    I couldn't stop myself.
Shouldn't someone enter the mind
of a teenager facing her final moments,

no one present, just her and the tree
her sliding toward proved powerless
to halt? Shouldn't someone think

of how she tried to lift her pinned arm,
of how she spoke her new child's name,
knowing she wouldn't live to hear

the ambulance arriving? What if,
in another time, we had turned one way
and not another? Isn't the story out of

our hands, revealed to us in small
moments, now and then an hour, a day,
a memory that keeps returning? Some

of their names I've carried decades, to no
real end, for no good reason other than
the weight of thinking of the absence

absence makes of them, of how we stay
a while, taking in as much as we
can bear, then pulling away, faces

staunch against what's left, the hopeless
inconsequential senseless familiar streets.

JEFF HARDIN

BEING IN YOUR OWN MIND

When you're with, say, your own kind,
those toward whom you do not feel

a need to prove yourself, to explain
the context out of which you speak;

being in your own mind's ease is easier then.
No fiddling to find the right word

to convey belief in sacramental places
like eddies along a creek's slow course

or underneath a sycamore's million leaves.
No need to think you need to craft an argument

for studying the stems of sapling oaks,
for following a hawk that holds itself aloft

along what's left of some horizon line.
Your own kind knows the things you know.

The way a cedar makes the soil acidic
and how a dogwood often grows nearby.

The way a wren builds decoy nests.
And how the men a generation back

would take it on themselves to stop and mend
a fence because they saw it needed done.

You used to think the mind could hold a truth,
but now you see the mind is like a walnut hull

before the vastness of the sky. The mind
is smaller than it thinks itself to be.

Sometimes you let your own heart be a hymn
nobody else can hear beneath your words.

It wanders like its Lord inside the coolness
of the day, and no one needs to know

to know the knowing it has come to know.
Not your kind, at least, who stand around

and nod agreement at the thing you didn't say
you didn't need to say because not saying it

is how you—your kind—sometimes let it say itself.

JEFF HARDIN

THE TENNESSEE KID

HAL CROWTHER

Photographs can mislead, and sometimes conceal more than they reveal. But on occasion, usually in hindsight, a photograph radiates so much insight you need sunglasses to examine it. A photograph in my college yearbook, circa 1962, shows a bunch of mugging freshmen engaged in the lame freshman humor that coat-and-tie group portraits traditionally provoked. Two turkeys in the back row are holding up a sign pilfered from a diner somewhere: "One Golden Brown Juicy Breast—with all the trimmings—89 cents."

Standing next to them, his torso half obscured by the juicy breast sign and a very strained look on his face, is a freshman from Memphis named James Ridout Winchester. You have to look carefully to confirm what you know for sure in hindsight, that it isn't Jimmy Winchester's hand holding up the left end of the breast sign. His hands appear to be deep in his pockets, and the sick look on his face says clearly, "Who are these people, and where am I, and why?" And this was in September, long before one of the six-month Siberian winters that drove more than one Southerner to transfer to Tulane.

It might be an understatement to say that Winchester was never comfortable at Williams College. Though a good fraternity welcomed him—he was a Tennessee thoroughbred with a pedigree that included Robert E. Lee—classmates never saw much of Jimmy. He was up in Bennington entertaining bohemian girls with blues chords, or he was on the road with his band, or rehearsing a rockabilly combo deep in the basement of the student union (if you sat quietly in the snack bar, you could just feel the beat). He lived off-campus with a divorced woman. Four years later, Winchester's senior yearbook photograph shows much longer hair and a still-quizzical expression. Beneath it, no honors or activities are listed, though one of the class musicians Jimmy used to play with listed a band called Roget and the Mojo Teeth.

Winchester wasn't the only one who experienced alienation in the Berkshire Mountains of New England. My hillbilly homesickness yielded slightly to an appetite for dead poets and distilled spirits, not necessarily in that order. From the beginning it was music that enabled Winchester to water his roots and endure his exile. He was from Memphis—a major South Memphis thoroughfare is Winchester Road—and most of us lacked the musical sophistication to grasp a fraction of what that implied. Elvis to be sure, but also Beale Street, B. B. King, Bobby Blue Bland, Sam Phillips and Sun Records, Booker T and the MGs. W. C. Handy was still living in Memphis when Jim Winchester was a teenager. When Handy died in 1958, Winchester's grandfather spoke at his funeral.

It was an unfair advantage. Where I grew up, live music was Salty Austin and the Allegheny Ridgerunners, aping Porter Wagoner. On weekdays Salty sold Electrolux vacuum cleaners door-to-door and left personalized guitar picks instead of calling cards. Once a month at American Legion Post 808, an emaciated, Baptist-looking woman named Audrey performed standards on the Hammond organ, backed up by her husband Pike, who looked anesthetized and played the drums with brushes. The culture gap between Sam Phillips and the Audrey/Pike ensemble might account for the discrepancy between Winchester's musical achievements and my own. But probably not.

"My mother tells me music was always my focus," Winchester recalled in 1999. "I studied piano all through grade school and high school, and I was always in a band with my friends, and I played the organ in church. But really, looking back, I always wanted to play guitar in an R&B band."

Going his own way, Winchester became a man of mystery at the college, the kind classmates tend to mythologize. I remember the rumors that he was in Boston or Springfield most weekends, opening shows for Taj Mahal. But a year out of Williams, after graduate study in Germany and a summer playing lounge piano in Memphis, Winchester took his myth to another level. His Vietnam draft notice came and he decamped for Montreal, guitar in hand—the only draft resister in the class, to my knowledge, who took the high road of emigration and public opposition to the war. The "Tennessee kid," as he calls himself in the classic "Brand New Tennessee Waltz," had committed himself to an exile that was neither academic nor symbolic.

"I was so young and naïve that it wasn't that difficult a decision," he said later. "I just wasn't thinking very far into the future."

The alumni grapevine works fast those first few years out of school. Winchester's departure was much discussed in New York. Most of us admired him for it. A couple of years after he moved to Montreal, a postcard of sorts arrived, a here's-how-I'm-doing that was characteristically original

The album photographs revealed that Jesse had a beard now and a lot more hair—quite a few of us had acquired beaucoup hair in the four years since graduation.

and myth-enriching. Jim was "Jesse Winchester" now, and that was the name of his debut album on the Bearsville label, produced by Robbie Robertson of The Band. "Jesse Winchester" introduced "The Brand New Tennessee Waltz," "Yankee Lady," and "Biloxi," three of the prettiest, subtlest, most mind-adhesive songs in the country-rock canon. They've been covered by so many singers that to this day they cover his alimony payments, as Jesse once told me mournfully.

The album photographs revealed that Jesse had a beard now and a lot more hair—quite a few of us had acquired beaucoup hair in the four years since graduation. He looked like a prophet; he had Robbie Robertson, Garth Hudson, and

Levon Helm for sidemen on his album; he knew Bob Dylan and Leonard Cohen. While his fraternity brothers were trying to pass their orals or make junior partner—while I was reviewing TV shows—Jesse was an international fugitive and a Canadian celebrity. He was light years ahead of the pack. And his songs were grand, to my ear—lyrical, ironic, simultaneously self-illuminating and self-deprecating. Smart, and full of displaced-Southerner angst.

"Now you know what they say about snowflakes," he mourns in "Snow," as another iron winter closes in. "How there ain't no two the same? Well, all them flakes look alike to me. Every one is a dirty shame."

"Jesse Winchester" backed up a wistful personal narrative with everything a boy soaked up in Memphis—blues, R&B, gospel, country, rock and rockabilly. Critics were uniformly impressed; performers and industry professionals were enthusiastic.

"As a collection of songs, the album is still nearly without peer," Herb Bowie wrote in an online review of Jesse's recordings, thirty-four years later.

"There was an intimacy in those songs that was new," recalls Barry Poss of Sugar Hill Records, which released two later Winchester albums (*Humor Me* in 1988 and *Gentleman of Leisure* in 1999). "It was a whole different take on love and loss."

"What my songs seem mainly to focus on is relationships with women or relationships with God," Winchester told an interviewer. "I tend to get those two confused."

Schoolmates who barely knew Jesse at Williams were suddenly his disciples. If his albums made small waves in the music industry, they made big ones in the class of '66. It's hard to invest much in the celebrity of adults we knew when they were children; we know them too well to buy into the mystique. But the separateness that Jesse always maintained—that was his trademark—allowed us to be his fans. There was a strange meeting in the late '70s that I always recall when I reflect on the paradox of celebrity. I went to hear Jesse play at The Pier in Raleigh, in the company of his old fraternity brother Bill Bennett, who was later to become Secretary of Education and federal drug czar under Ronald Reagan—and eventually the self-appointed guardian of America's morals, until a hemorrhaging addiction to high-stakes gambling cost him his pulpit.

Bennett, too, is a great character, of a less endearing variety. The three of us sat backstage after Jesse's show, in a tiny dressing room that reeked of cigarettes, making awkward small talk about undergraduate adventures. Bennett and I were unconditionally impressed with Winchester; for his part he was impeccably gracious but seemed to find us almost as bewildering as those freshmen with the juicy breast sign in 1962. Bennett and I were both becoming pontificators—of radically different types, I hope—and Jesse was an artist born, a different animal. I know what I think of Bennett; I'm fairly sure I know what Winchester thought of him, too. I had no idea what Jesse thought of me.

There's a distinct male pecking order where musicians rule; you're tone-deaf if you think William Bennett, who once aspired to the presidency of the United States, was the celebrity in that little room. Bennett himself would never make that claim. Like me, like the rest of us, he probably followed the rest of Jesse's career as avidly as Memphis kids followed Elvis.

It's been an uneven, almost unclassifiable career. Winchester became a Canadian citizen in 1973. When Jimmy Carter pardoned the Vietnam draft resisters in 1977, a friend called Jesse in Canada, and he remembers that he "just sat down on the bed and wept, I was so moved." But he kept faith with the Maple Leaf, with the country that welcomed him when America had no peaceful use for him. He lived most of his adult life in Quebec and raised three children there, for years in the Eastern Townships, seventy hard winter miles from Montreal.

Though no less an authority than Bob Dylan calls him one of the best singer-songwriters of his generation—Dylan's generation—the conventional wisdom is that exile deprived Jesse of a chance to be a star.

"His early inability to tour in the U.S. may have permanently stunted his commercial success," speculated Herb Bowie. Jesse's stock never traded briskly on the celebrity exchange; *People* magazine, a founder of that grim exchange, said of Winchester in February of 1989, "He certainly seems too obscure for a performer of his talent."

In 1990 Jesse announced his retirement as a performer and recorded nothing for a decade. When he returned in 1999 with Sugar Hill's *Gentleman of Leisure*, his obscurity had become a theme. In a piece headed "The Return of Jesse Winchester" in the *Toronto Star*, Nick Krewen described an artist "whose stature, through ten albums and 28 years has always been more satellite than star, orbiting the peripheral [*sic*] between respectability and reverence."

"Album sales have been nominal," Krewen added.

Jesse himself made black humor of his meager renown, with a streak of self-mockery prefigured by his second album, *Third Down, 110 to Go*. He recalled opening for Jimmy Buffett and singing one of his own songs that Buffett had recorded. "The audience was annoyed because they thought I was singing one of Jimmy's songs," he said. "It's kind of the story of my life."

The image industry isn't everything—in an age of Britney Spears, Donald Trump, and *American Idol* it's a pretty dismal business. While his career appeared to languish, Winchester's songs were recorded by a formidable lineup of discriminating A-list artists including Joan Baez, the Everly Brothers, Waylon Jennings, Bonnie Raitt, Emmylou Harris, Reba McEntire, Elvis Costello and Wynonna Judd. The attention dried up but not the money. Unlike some great blues artists who had more lean years than fat, Winchester never had to load trucks or play lodge picnics to make ends meet. But he became one of those cult figures who separates serious music buffs from the day-trippers. Everyone knowledgeable knew *who* he was, but almost no one knew *where* he was.

By paying close attention I managed several Winchester sightings over the years, every one rewarding. One night in the mid-'80s my wife and I caught up with him at Rhythm Alley in Chapel Hill, North Carolina, for a set highlighted by a

Unlike some great blues artists who had more lean years than fat, Winchester never had to load trucks or play lodge picnics to make ends meet.

remarkable live version of Jesse's funky "Rhumba Man." ("My step might be old-fashioned/But it's just fine with me/I got a couple of rhumba steps/You might like to see.")

Here was a skinny, incongruously formal guy with a neatly trimmed beard, dressed like an off-duty librarian, performing a weird soft-shoe shuffle like your Uncle Dan might assay after his third martini. But you quickly saw the art of it. No hoofer, no athlete, Winchester just had those Beale Street rhythms coiled around his bones, and his exhibition of fancy footwork was one of the most arresting novelties in show business. If you're thinking Savion Glover, move along. If you love the Rabbit Dance performed by Too Slim Riders in the Sky—who also played Rhythm Alley—"Rhumba Man" live might have been your personal epiphany.

Backstage alone, reserved as always but with his Southern manners fine-tuned by the presence of a lady, Jesse seemed genuinely glad to see us. The last time I talked to him, he was working my favorite bluegrass festival, Doc Watson's MerleFest in North Wilkesboro, North Carolina. With all the credentials he carried—Memphis, Montreal, Nashville, political dissent, the imprimatur of Dylan and The Band—you'd think Jesse might have worked up some kind of hip look for himself, at least onstage, at least surrounded by so many musicians in their righteous gear. Instead he performed in a V-neck sweater, striped button-down shirt, chinos, and penny loafers—a uniquely retro costume borrowed from a small-town history teacher, or one of our more conservative preppies at Williams long ago.

Graying now, playing alone on a vintage guitar, Jesse made our day—the few of us, the ones who knew—with a low-key set of familiar, beautifully crafted songs. Backstage he was abstracted, shy, a wayfaring stranger who didn't seem to know anyone—still an exile, as he sang and wrote, "with my feet in Dixie and my head in the cool blue North."

The class grapevine is fraying now; there are a lot of missing links in the network, one way or another. Classmates have died, of course; another one reached Jesse by e-mail to ask him if he might be interested in performing at the fortieth reunion of the class of 1966. The predictable answer was a polite but resounding "No thanks." Not even Barry Poss, who recorded Jesse, could ever tell me exactly where to find him, though he knew people who might know, he said. The only clues were on Jesse's website. Once it listed a three-show tour in Northern California—Petaluma (McNear's Mystic Theater), Saratoga, Santa Cruz—that coincided exactly with a trip I made to Death Valley. But those east-west roads in the desert aren't so good, and I felt way too old to drive across the Sierra Nevadas at night, even to see Jesse Winchester. There was no hurry, it seemed to me. The Rhumba Man was out there somewhere, and somewhere we'd meet again. I was wrong. In 2014 I got a call from a friend in New York, a classmate who had once played the drums in Jesse's band. His news was that Winchester, back in the States since 2002, had died of cancer at his home in Charlottesville, just short of his seventieth birthday. I thought of some lines from "The Brand New Tennessee Waltz": "Let all of your passionate violins play a tune for a Tennessee kid/Who's thinking of leaving another town, with no place to go if he did/They'll catch you wherever you're hid." ■

HALM AVE, LOS ANGELES

1965: Sandy Koufax hurls
fastballs that crackle
like limp-wristed
copper wires swaying
above the lawn. My father,
only nine, lips raw from pineapple,
dances in rhythm
to the transistor radio
blaring on the sidewalk.

Koufax shakes off Roseboro.
My father's coke bottle glasses
fall into brown glass.
He comes set.
Hands that will punch
a man for smoking in a mine shaft
and feet that will ache
from steel-toed boots, silent.
The delivery.
The left arm flails,
the right leg lifts to his chest.
He falls into the grass, laughing.
Sandy paints the corner, strike three.

It is 1965 and my father is nine,
miming the motions of perfection,
not yet knowing the echoes of Watts,
where cars flamed and National Guardsmen
shot at boys six years older.
Though he choked on coal-dust
and skunked UMW beer,

he is always nine, tearing up dead sod,
barely beating the tag,
a belly-flop across home.

ERIC JANKEN

SUMMERTIME CHI

Short for Chicago

From a rooftop on Lincoln Ave.
          you can see the fountain fill with angel wings.
Summer's humid cape trails
          your bike through grid-pattern streets.

Windblown, lake effect, rain-washed leaves.
          Jazz music means: Uptown, red line.
Train window. I believe
          this city belongs to me, and Capone
still ghost-tags rooftop burners.

I love the hijacked look of a girl
          on the subway as she loses her balance,
and reaches for the bar. This is how
          you learn to love again.

In Chicago, blue hue on sun brick.
          Flashlight beams rope through dark apartments,
a police cruiser jumps the curb.
          You might overhear, "I marched
with Zombies last night."

From the el, watch it zip by:
          fixie in Logan Square,
Jungle smoke-stained avenues,
          the spirt of Nelson Algren,
the spirit of the stockyard,
          transplants emerging from tunnels.

You can find your way in the summertime.

Then, I see my own breath,
        stumbling down the sidewalk with you,
on a cool night, catching a cab,
        cause the bus is blocks away.

And tomorrow, we'll ride the rails
        and the sun will crest the lake.
And the body count will grow
        and glow like neon in the rain.

BRYCE BERKOWITZ

AN *APPALACHIAN HERITAGE* CONVERSATION WITH

BELL HOOKS & FENTON JOHNSON

When *Appalachian Heritage* hosted a conversation between bell hooks and Fenton Johnson in April, the two native Kentuckians spoke to a packed house filled with students, professors, community members, and even a couple who had driven in from Texas specially for the event. After Johnson read from his recently published essay collection titled

Everywhere Home, the two celebrated writers began a dialogue that was both thought-provoking and revelatory.

Over the course of an hour, they divulged stories of their parallel lives and identities as queer Kentuckians who left the region for California, and recounted how they each found solace in solitude as writers and individuals. Although they did not know each other until recently, they have since found a connection in the threads of their lives and in their identity as outsiders to their communities.

In this edited conversation, hooks and Johnson discuss defining borders, generational shifts, the current political moment, and the importance of silence in a world of technology in which nothing ever seems to pause.

■ ■ ■

bell hooks: Fenton and I have had a very curious parallel Kentucky experience. We both left Kentucky and went to Stanford [University]. We both saw California as a kind of promised land, and we did not encounter each other even though we were in the same class at Stanford, but serendipitously we have come together at this stage of our life. Fenton has been writing amazing stuff about solitude, about the importance and value of solitude.

Fenton Johnson: [I wrote] a cover essay ["Going It Alone"] in *Harper's* about three years ago. I'm supposed to be turning it into a book even as we speak. It will be called *At the Center of All Beauty*, which is a line from a Frank O'Hara poem. I define solitude very broadly, because I have known people—I'm clear that I'm not talking about hermits, although I respect hermits for what it is that they're doing—but these are [people] who have a kind of sense of aloneness that is inherent to them.

So many people can manage to be solitaries in marriage. In fact I would say the marriages that I admire and respect the most are the marriages that fall into what the critic Phyllis Rose called "parallel lives," where two people agree to be solitaries together. Marianne Moore has a poem called "Marriage," in which one person says to another I should like to be alone, and the other person says, I should like to be alone, too. Why not be alone together? I was going to use *Alone Together* as the title of this book until I found out that somebody else had already used it.

Then I had another cover essay in *Harper's* that...came out [in January 2018] which is called "The Future of Queer," in which I argue that we all need to become queer because of where the culture as a whole is going right now and that it's a useful definition.

bh: Yes. Well, I mean one of the ways that we got to be so queer is [by] precisely [recognizing] ourselves as outsiders in the family and the culture that we were raised in, and therefore spending lots of time in our heads, in our imagination, and that's where we still land. That's [what seems to be behind your book] *Everywhere Home*. Everywhere home for us is the imagination, is the experience of writing and creating.

FJ: Isn't that nice to think of home? I'd like to point out that home is a concept that really only exists in English—it's a concept that is pretty unique to the English language. In fact I don't think any other language has the word that we carry that has such richness and associations. In French you can say *chez moi*, which is "at my house," but it doesn't have those kinds of connotations that the word "home" does. Isn't it nice to think that, in fact, home is a product of the imagination, and as I say towards the end of this collection of essays, "How would we treat the world if we treated everywhere as home?" If we treated the strip mine site and the Superfund site in New Jersey and Love Canal—whatever, take your pick, the Olana River, the Kentucky River. How would we really treat those if we thought of each of those as home rather than home as something that has a border around it?

bh: Both of us left Kentucky in search of a world where we could more fully belong, as outsiders, as queer, as not being like everybody else.

FJ: Yeah. I just read Lidia Yuknavitch['s] book called *The Misfit's Manifesto*...I disagree with some of the things that she says in that book. [But] she has a great moment where she says that those of us who, I would say, are queer—we define the space that includes everybody else, that you have to go to the margins or the borders of your way of thinking. Conventionality is what occupies the big space in between, but it's the borders that define that, and the people who define those borders are the people who are the edgy, interesting, sometimes dangerous thinkers.

bh: When I thought about [the title of] my book *Feminist Theory: From Margin to Center*, it was precisely that sense of how being an outsider can actually influence the center in ways that are counter-hegemonic.

FJ: I think ultimately what happens over and over again is that the ideas that are outrageous to one generation become the accepted ideas of the next generation. So would you rather be digging your heels in, or would you rather be an agent of change? I don't mean that as a simple and obvious question because there are certainly values that need to be carried forward in one fashion or another. I have to imagine that

Fenton Johnson

many people of the Trump Revolution would see themselves as radical agents of change, but you can figure that one out for yourself. I think it is a matter of character, and it is one of the things that I'm writing about in this book on solitaries.

There's a certain character that has difficulty. One discovers that one has difficulty fitting in from the first and that that is somehow contained in historical circumstance, in the moment in history that you're born into, and then also what the essayist Phillip Lopate calls—a phrase I really love—the "catastrophe of character." Each of us is subject to the "catastrophe of character," which is that part of ourselves that we call character, [which] is who we are. It is what we are, and we act out of it.

bh: It's interesting that we both come from large families. He's one of nine. I'm one of seven. That sense of being in a community that you haven't chosen but that seeks to contain you. That's an experience that I think both you and I have struggled with and against.

FJ: Yeah, I think [it's] one of the things that's interesting about Kentucky. I have wandered far, but my mother was alive until June of last year. She died at 101 years old, so I was involved in coming back to be part of her caregiving quite a bit. But I had a friend once who said to me—he's from Oklahoma, a Stanford friend—"You know, I left Oklahoma as fast as I could," and once his parents died, because they did, "I will never go back. I have no interest in going back there at all, and yet everybody I knew from Kentucky is always talking about going back. What is that about?" And that's an interesting question. It's true. I think one of the things that draws us back is that intensity of connection to place.

Fenton Johnson's book, *Everywhere Home.*

bh: My sense of queerness really came from Kentucky and from the backwoods people that were my relatives who had a very particular take on life. I think that that's one of the reasons some of us return, because we find that grounding in otherness, in being queer—past gay, because it has nothing to do with being gay. So many of us actually got that in Kentucky, got that within those families that were trying both to contain us and at times destroy us. I mean my mother would say to me, "You're mine, and I'll kill you if I want to"—that whole sense of possession of self and identity. I always remember that I got smacked for saying, "I don't have a mother." There again is that notion of kind of being an alien who's just giving birth to herself.

FJ: Well, I certainly know that [as the youngest] I was my mother's acting out of her dreams—she wanted [to leave], she would love to have gone. I asked once what she wanted to do if she hadn't married and founded a library in New Haven, Kentucky, and she said, "Move to South America and become a tango dancer." I had gone to California and I'd went to New York, and I took this job at the University of Arizona, and she said, "What are you going to do in Arizona?" and I said, "I'm going to be a professor," and she said, "Oh, a professor." That was acceptable.

I wrote an essay called "Catholic in the South"...that opens with a line of tribute to my father. I'll tell first this little anecdote: I wanted to kind of fact check [the piece]. You know, I had the *New York Times* [looking] over my shoulder, so I went to my oldest sister, and I said, "Do you remember our father saying this line?" And she said, "Well, I don't remember him saying it, but it's true, and if he didn't say it, he ought to have said it." The line was: "Catholics are like muskrats. They never venture far from water," which is really true. Catholics choose water, along the Ohio River, down the Mississippi, along Great Lakes, on the coasts.

Anyway, that essay ends with my writing and thinking of the Catholic Church, and thinking of the South, and I've come to understand that this is what they share: "an uncompromising demand that they be accepted on their terms. It is exactly because they demand our loves wholly and unconditionally that we find them so hard to leave behind, that they draw us back in spite of ourselves. In this age of relativism, few places can, and few people do."

bh: And I keep saying to him that he needs to come on back to Kentucky. Do you think being gay in Kentucky is different [than from other places]?

FJ: Boy, isn't that a good question? There are certainly people who could answer that question more authoritatively than I. You know, I think one thing. I seriously considered buying my mother's house because I could, and because my job as the youngest—my father harvested bricks out of old bourbon warehouses that were back in the woods, little family establishments, and my job was...to knock the mortar off of the bricks so we could use the bricks to build the house. And Seagram's had been using cypress tubs to age the mash in, and they replaced them with stainless steel tubs, so my father took all that cypress and planed it down and made tongue-and-groove paneling for the whole house, so the whole house smelled like the inside of a mash tub for the first fifteen years that we lived in it. There is an enormous stone, this piece of limestone...that was where they would tie up the draft horses. That was our picnic table in the backyard. My mother built a greenhouse [in]1958, to raise orchids and cactus.

It's quite a place, but then I think about being a single gay man in New Haven...I'll tell another story which is not a happy story. I was a sophomore in high school or maybe a junior, and the boys were riding around, and part of the fun of that evening was to go find a house where a man lived alone. And because he lived alone, therefore, he must be queer or strange or odd. I'm happy to say I did not join, but the entertainment for the evening was to gather a bunch of rocks and throw it at this guy's house. I think if I lived alone in New Haven, Kentucky, somebody would heave a brick through my window. I think that would still happen. Am I wrong about that?

bh: Well, it certainly probably wouldn't happen in Berea, even though we can't seem to bring ourselves to pass the fairness initiative [that would provide protections in public accomodations on the basis of sexual orientation and gender identity].

FJ: We all have to mention the current political moment. I was flying through Dallas to come here, and President Trump was on the TV...and there were two people watching...who had a kind of—I don't know a word to use other than beatific expression on their faces. And I thought, *is this the moment that five years from now I will look back and say, "This is when Hitler came to power"?* There were people who [were] totally unquestioning, totally under [his] power.

And then, driving from Louisville this morning, there was a lawn maintenance truck, and it was doing the speed limit [and] the police pulled it over. I thought, *I wonder if they're pulling that truck over because lawn maintenance*—"we're going to check the papers of the people in there." We're in a moment where they can do that, just to harass those people. I think we all have to get out there and fight. It's a really critical moment, don't you think?

bell hooks

bh: Absolutely.

FJ: I want to ask this question: [what was] the process that led your decision to come back?

bh: My decision to come back to Kentucky really had to do with my relationship to my parents and the fact that I knew they were closer to dying than they would ever be to—as my father said, "Gloria, I'm not going up the mountain. I'm coming down the mountain." It's always struck me as particularly Kentucky, that his metaphors for his life were about mountains and hills which is where we were raised, you know, the hills of Kentucky. That sense of return. I, of course, have always felt very strongly about my family in Kentucky and how to hold onto that and be an outsider and be a queer person in the world, and it has become easier to be that difference.

I was [recently] inducted into the Kentucky Writers Hall of Fame. What was odd about [the ceremony] and intriguing is that the other [inducted] writers, for the most part, were very into the Confederacy, so that there was kind of this odd blend of the old with a new vision of Kentucky, of the progressive people that I actually believe have always been in Kentucky but that get no play. I mean, my grandparents weren't people who were reading and writing [but] they lived these amazingly creative lives. You know, my grandmother sold fishing worms. That was her big thing. All of those things are kind of our buried stories of difference and otherness in Kentucky.

For me, one [reason] why I could return to Kentucky is because the rest of the world was becoming as crazy as Kentucky. The things that I was fleeing when I left Kentucky—you know the racism, the white supremacy—all of those things were just becoming the norm in places like New York, or all of these places where...I mean, it's interesting to think about how gentrification, whenever it takes place in cities, is usually about whiteness, privileged whites moving and pushing out people of color. I think back to the black farmers in Kentucky whose lands were just taken from them by white people who would just show up and burn the house down or what have you. That's kind of what's happening in our culture as a whole now. So, it's like, why should you miss out on the good things in Kentucky because of evil, because the evil is everywhere?

FJ: On a positive note, this is why this place is so important—why places like this are so important—is because the otherness that you describe is the fertile ground for the imagination. And it is the act of the imagination that enables us to understand that the other person whose experiences are so different from my experiences and who looks so different from me, is at heart a human being who wants happiness in the way that I do, perhaps under different language or different whatever, but that the difference, the otherness, is a source of richness as anybody who practices any kind of art form would know. You go to that place to find what it is that's going to make your work particularly interesting or engaging. [I'm reminded of] that quotation from André Gide in which he says, We're always trying to find the thing in us that is different and to smooth it out and eliminate it and destroy it when in fact that's the thing that really makes us who we are. Figuring out ways to cultivate that difference and to encourage that difference, I think, is what places like this are about, [places] like Appalshop [the artistic media collective based in Whitesburg, Kentucky].

bh: That's why I encourage you to return for a time. ■

WHAT WE TELL OURSELVES

I.
I show him my pay stub my weekly deposit
slip reasons for needing ten dollars   this is
how it has to be This
                                    is working nine hour days
on my feet barely a break to come home
cook sweep mop wash wait
on him This
                                    is watching it fall around me
him sitting while shingles fly with every wind
gutters hanging loose leaking the back porch
needing the new gate This is him
                                                        watching me
while I push mow rake leaves rake limbs this is him
this is his and I have no business asking
for help or money   I shouldn't expect him to

the woman's place is to submit this
is fitting to the Lord

II.
[You can walk away
                                    and not look back]

III.
I'm too tired It's too expensive It was
his time to go I'll pray for you I had no
idea this was coming I've never raised
my voice or a hand to her She
has another feller The water is safe

Things are different
for a girl You can't do that I won't
let you I will knock your head off
I will take your car keys Do you
hear me I don't want to I'm not able to
She's wanted this for a long time She
asked for it
                                        deep down
I come by it natural I come by it honest

IV.
[You can stay
            and survive]

V.
You'll never get married if you can't handle a man
wailin' on you   if you don't change
your attitude   don't shut up   don't
wear more dresses make up   if you don't learn to cook
don't stop being bossy   you better stop trying to show
how smart you are   stop tearing your legs up
playing sports, men like legs   stop sleeping
in sports bras, men like big breasts like your mother's
things are different for a girl   whatever this is
                                          you'd better get over it

VI.
[You can leave]

VII.

I never wanted to stay I never wanted to
leave I never wanted to come back to gravel dust
I could not wait to leave I could not breathe
in the shadows I could not stand
the good country boys could not stand
the bible-thumping teenage girl humping
men I never could keep a secret
their shit-eating grins scratch-my-back politics
I know I will never meet people
as honey-suckle good as home
I know city neighbors won't never love me
as much I know what the good country
people say I know the good curvy road
I know how my skin tightens
when I have to go home I don't want to
go home I don't know where
home is I don't know if I love
the mountains I don't know if I hate
the mountains I love to drown
in the mountains I hate the crooked
mountains I love the mountains I hate
the mountains I love the mountains I hate
the mountains I love

VIII.

[It's a choice]

IX.

On the long dry days I wish I had hit you
I wish I had reared back as you screamed
I'll knock your damned teeth out
I wish I had let it fly I wish I'd

cocked my fist to your jaw right
as you claimed
I'll do it   *I will*

On those days I wake with the copper taste
of hate in my mouth When I can't
sweat it out cold I can't hold it
under the creek of me
I know I don't know
which I hate more
your lack of follow-
through or my own

X.
[Our anger is a lantern This little light
of mine]

XI.
Hang it in the family room:

> *Man puts his hand to the flinty rock*
> *and overturns mountains by the roots.*
> *He cuts out the channels in the rocks,*
> *and his eye sees every precious thing.*
> *He dams up the streams so that they do*
> *not trickle,*
> *and the thing that is hidden he brings*
> *out to light.*
>
> *But where shall wisdom be found?*

XII.
[It's our fault]

XIII.
Rid her of topsoil   cleanse the skin
blast it open with knife   with dynamite
[The things we mine out are what kill us]
Needlewire your way to the seam   dragline tissue
swift   strive for clean margins   Place small clips
metal clips to mark your spoil   Don't over burden
her with waste   use a drain for the slurry
What would we save if we didn't destroy   the breast
Follow up with sponge baths support groups
radiation bumper stickers Then you can
reclaim what is yours

XIV.
[You can come back]

XV.
She always was a little bit quare they'll say
when you show up at the funeral home
with a full-on lezzie pompadour
black dress and tights be damned.
Still you'll smile and tell them you're doing
just fine   even after the good church folks
stare at you side-eyed and whisper *backslider.*

XVI.
[You can forgive]

XVII.
When it all goes to hell, the holiest
among them turn on you first   will
open a red-spined hymnal   sing
It is well [it is well] with my soul [with my soul]
It is well it is well with my soul.

XVIII.
[It's not our fault]

XIX.
Once the mountains loved us. Once we loved the mountains.

SAVANNAH SIPPLE

[JESUS RIDES SHOTGUN]

We go balls to the wall,
windows down,
aviator sunglasses always on.
I drive like a bat
out of hell, do donuts
on sun-dry highways,
180s on ice-slick parkways. Sometimes
when I drift, I think
this is the end.

I used to be afraid. Sometimes
I still am. Maybe.

Don't hit the brakes, Jesus says.
Turn the wheel. That's how you know
the way you want to go.

SAVANNAH SIPPLE

MAXIMS
IN WINTER

LOIS WOLFE

Ida walked the length of her backyard in old tennis shoes, holding a thin sweater tight against her ribs. The dew on the grass made her toes cold. She planted a foot at the edge of the muddy plot she had gardened and leaned in over the garden, trying to find a bright spot at the center of the mess.

There lay the cukes, prickly and pithy, bittering themselves. A few beans hung limp in thinning leaves, runners tangled on a trellis made of rusty chicken wire. The bottom half of her last ripening tomato had been gnawed and left to ruin, thanks to the groundhog that lived under the empty doghouse at the far end of the yard. She had tried poisoning his burrow in the spring but all she got was a pile of black moles. Moles had eaten the grubs that ingested the poison and then died in a heap of star-nosed little bodies, an organizing of corpses, which she attributed to the neighbor's tomcat who didn't even have the grace to eat one and die. The cat was a daily eyesore. The groundhog haunted only when he pleased and ruined only what interested him. He was a ghost she did not know how to get rid of.

Ida moved to the other side of the garden plot so that she could feel better, standing alongside her corn. Corn was tall. The stalks had pretty golden hair. Corn made a garden look like it was doing something of stature. Not this year. All she had were stunted ears on bent stalks, silks wizened black. Sweet corn was just a name on a seed packet anyway, Ida thought. There was no guarantee.

She navigated rickety steps to get to the back porch and entered her cramped kitchen from the mudroom her husband, Hemmel, had insisted on adding. It was the German in him. Ida could have done with a bigger porch instead of a mudroom the size of an outhouse but she was a get-along person in those days, not the prickly piece of work she was now. Her favorite granddaughter, Jean Marie, would not have recognized the meek woman she had been. Jean Marie was only fourteen and had only known Ida as a widowed grandma. Hemmel had been dead twenty-three years. A stroke took him the week before his fifty-fourth birthday. Ida had learned that being a widow was a trickier proposition than it seemed. It freed a woman of the good of a man as well as the bad. In the end, death appeared just as confused as the widows it left behind. It mistook which parts of a man to bury.

Jean Marie was at an eager age to zero in on those kinds of oops in the logic of life. Ida had learned to be wary when her granddaughter visited. The girl was an experienced detective of the heart. Teenagers heard the taint in any truth adults tried to talk their way around. Worse, they lacked the grace to accept necessary lies.

"For goodness sake, Jean Marie. I'm not losing my house. It's a tax bill. I'm going to pay it."

"Mom said they're going to be knocking on your door to evict you if you're not careful."

"Your mom's exaggerating. She's trying to make a drama out of a little piece of paper from that Tax Collector I didn't even vote for. He's a Republican. Got those soft hands. Pudgy. They get that way."

"Grammy, you were having a breakdown. The doctor had to give you tranquilizers. Mom said you were going to take a shotgun to the clerk that brought the papers."

"Perty's too dramatic. Sorely mistaken, too." Ida took a seat in the rocker facing a window that looked out on the backyard and the sorry garden. "All I did was stand the gun by my chair here and let that leech from the tax office know it's for groundhogs, which it is." Ida nodded firmly. "I do not break down."

Ida knew she was good at this. She'd had a lifetime of deciding which failings to hide when. Lately, though, the effort of choosing the right thing to conceal at the right time seemed to cost more concentration than she could afford and she had taken to talking to people sideways. That way, she didn't have to worry whether her eyes were showing a truth or half-truth. For flat-out lies, she was safe. She had a special look fixed straight ahead to the edge of infinity where no one could follow her.

"What kind of medicine did the doctor give you, then?"

"Flu pills. I had the flu. Probably still have it, so don't get close."

Jean Marie came around the chair and leaned her butt on the window sill, facing Ida. Ida fixed a look out the window beyond the edge of everything she knew because the prescription was for nerve pills. Taking one had made her numb to the world so she poured the rest into the groundhog burrow, trying to put that dumb animal to sleep for good.

"For goodness sake." Ida rocked her chair so far forward she crowded Jean Marie off the sill and off to the side, out of a direct line of sight. "The flu is just piffle. It's not like I've been struck low with stroke or cancer or failure of a vital organ like the pancreas. Never underestimate your pancreas, Jean Marie. It's small but tricky. You need to keep up your guard against little slippery things that do their job in the dark."

"Is that a maxim? I have to come up with twenty-five of them before school starts." She rolled her eyes with more pride than disgust. "I'm in eighth grade now."

Ida didn't know what Jean Marie was talking about so she ignored the question and made a little show of feeling parched and signaled for a glass of water. Ida had dropped out of school in the eighth grade and every day since, she had expected a reminder of that fact to pop up in the form of an unknown word, a smart-aleck person, or a question she couldn't answer. And there it was for today, from her favorite granddaughter, no less.

Jean Marie began to talk slower and louder, as if Ida was deaf. "A maxim is a piece of advice that sounds wise. It's short but it means something longer and stronger," she said. "It makes a person sound smart about things. I need you to help me sound smart for Missus Porter."

"She's your new teacher?"

"Homeroom and history. Kids say she's a real crab."

"That's a shame. She was a Wilford, you know, a gleeful people. They danced and played fiddles in the yard. Lived up in Crow Hollow where it was steep as a teacup and hard to farm. God gave them a butt-ugly piece of land and no money but they never stopped smiling. Then that teacher of yours married Old Man Porter, got fat and turned into a crab. That's what education does for you."

"That's gossip, not a maxim. Tell me something that's short and sweet and builds character."

"Life is not a box of Mini-Wheats, Jean Marie. You can't get it dropped sugar-frosted in a princess bowl, one square at a time."

"Admit it. You don't have a maxim, not a one."

"What I don't have is time to lay out all the things a girl needs to know in two weeks before school starts."

"Really, Grammy? All you have is time."

"That's insulting." Ida busied herself with the fold of the afghan across her belly. She looked through the window at her backyard bordered by the ugly mildewed fence that hid her ugly prune-faced neighbor, Bernice. "I run out of time everyday. Look out there. No time to whitewash that plank fence."

"Daddy offered to pressure wash it for you this summer."

Ida ignored the reminder. "I don't have time to stack firewood on my porch, either."

"Your flue's stopped up. You'd burn the house down. Mom told you no wood until you let Dad clean that flue."

"Like I don't know how to burn wood with a dirty flue. In all our years, Hemmel never cleaned a chimney once."

"He never had to. Mom says you moved every year."

Oh, the places he had found for them, the squalor she had cleaned. Hemmel had always sent Ida ahead to absorb the emptiness, cover the soiled and stained, and hide evidence from the girls, Perty and Rose—that their family was just another link in the chain of desperate lives taking cover until they were pushed out. Until this house. Here they'd stayed put. It had been a miracle, at the time.

Ida shrugged. "Rent money was tight."

"Mom doesn't talk much about hardships. She talks about your grit, how strong you were. She says you're resourceful."

The thought of Perty talking about her like that made Ida smile without moving a muscle on her face. "I like my hardships," she said, settling her lap robe. "They keep me warm."

Jean Marie refilled Ida's water glass and set it dripping on the sill by Ida's chair. "School gave us a recorder to share for the summer and, tomorrow, Joey Roneska has to give me my turn to use it."

"Roneska's are tight. They don't give much. They come over from the Old Country and they got two ways of saying everything. That's what knowing two languages can do for you. Doubles every bad word out of your mouth. Pretty damn handy."

"When I come back with that recorder, you better have something respectable to say."

"What I'm going to say, little Caesar, is stop strutting around my house on those chubby knees giving orders. "

Jean Marie groaned and tugged her T-shirt lower to cover her belly. "I'm not chubby." She flopped into a chair. "I'm fat."

Ida instantly regretted her candor. "Don't be silly. That's not fat when you're fourteen. It's worry waddles. We all had'em. Worried that things got tucked all wrong with too much here, not enough there. Next year, you'll stretch it all out. Next year, everything just shifts into place. Count on that, Jean Marie. You come from good stock. You've got that straight Munzer nose. Good cheekbones. Classy hands, small and thin. Shiny black Cherokee hair, like your mother. But that's not why you're a wonder. It's because you're the only child that listens. Listening is an art, Jean Marie. Hearing is nothing. Your mother's heard me all her life."

"You two make me sick, picking at each other. How come you're always fighting?"

"We're not fighting. We don't have a chance. We don't hardly see each other."

"You fight with Mom every time you see me. You think I'm going to repeat everything you say about her. No, m'am. I don't come here to carry back insults."

Ida was afraid of the answer but had to ask. "Why do you come here?"

"Because people shake their head when I say I'm your granddaughter and I don't know what it means. Maybe they pity me. Or they pity you. Or they're just thinking what a lip you got on you and I'm probably going to have one on me, too. Whatever it is making people shake their head, Gram, spit it out."

"I don't know what people think. Don't care, neither."

"Then talk about what you do know. Make maxims, a whole bunch of them so I can pick the best. And you better have a good one about being a grandmother because you really need to read it."

Jean Marie left looking tight, like a fist. It was not natural. Ida was not ready for Jean Marie to grow up angry.

Maybe that's the first maxim a granddaughter should know, Ida thought. A child's natural state is not being balled up like that. The natural position is listing, leaning toward something with an open mind, ready to grasp. Children are born to grasp. Most children. Jean Marie's older sister, Diane, bless her bleached blonde heart, would not list forward into anything Ida had to say. Diane could turn away looking straight at you, she was that rude. Then there was the boy,

Bucky. Never got close. He cottoned to the other grandma. Dex saw to that.

Jean Marie was the one with a curious soul and honest eye. She leaned into Ida's words with a neat tilt of chin and rise-up of caterpillar-brown brows that made her eyes seem bigger, more expectant. Sometimes, Ida had to stop and fall silent when Jean Marie listed. There was too much room in her granddaughter's eyes. Ida didn't believe they could be filled by an old woman's teasing and idle talk about the stories of her day. Sometimes Ida just wanted to stop and tell the truth. *I'm not enough, Jean Marie.*

Sleeping at night had become an iffy proposition. Ida gave up and rose at 4 a.m. the next day, percolated a half-pot of coffee and waited by the window for light to break so that she could see the stories of the day. The first was The Tomcat

There was too much room in her granddaughter's eyes. Ida didn't believe they could be filled by an old woman's teasing and idle talk about the stories of her day.

Fails Again, her favorite. Her neighbor's tomcat was a big grey with a pudgy head and oily fur, trying to sneak up on young chickadees in the laurel bush. Two older birds spotted him and made a warning ruckus but the cat just crept lower in the grass, getting closer to the trunk of the tree. Then a bird from a higher perch dove like a loosed arrow and stabbed the cat in his flank. He yowled and recoiled. Chickadees joined in with fast looping strikes at the tom's head, a fat target for tiny beaks. The cat ran back to his own yard, flicking his head, trying to get the sting out. Tomcat fails again. Serves him right, and his old biddy, Bernice, too.

Another story started up and she leaned close to the window. She called it Tool Man Turns It On. It was her other neighbor, Fletch, who revved up power tools at daybreak. Today it was his self-propelled mower, taking another eighth inch off of grass that didn't need cut. Funny, what comforts a man. She rarely saw him but heard his tools going all the time. Funny, what comforted her. She didn't need to talk with Fletch as long as she knew he was there making noise. Snip of the shears meant hedge-work. Hack of the hoe in soft dirt was weed-killing. Squeak of an old plunger gun was bugs in the beans and a rising fog of 8-10-10. She had had bugs in her beans, too, but she was too proud to ask him to spray. Her garden had been a shameful enterprise this year. She couldn't take care of anything and wouldn't have a respectable vegetable to show for the season.

Honestly, what did she have to show for any season?

Ida hunted the answer so seriously and deeply that she must have knocked over a pillar in her inner temple of common sense. She found herself doing something that her family would have found crazy. All alone, she said her name aloud. "Ida Ellen Munzer."

It came out raggedy, uncertain. She cleared her throat and said it distinctly, as if she were speaking into a tape recorder or sitting on the witness stand in a courtroom. "Ida Ellen Munzer."

She struggled to prepare for Jean Marie. She fought the arthritis in her lower back and inched herself out of the rocking chair. At the kitchen table, under a plastic bread bag holding two stale heels, she found a Bic pen. A ring-bound notebook lay on the pecan sofa table that Hemmel had bought from some Pennsylvania Mennonites on one of his last away trips. Her husband had been an insurance salesman who preferred tri-state territories. In fact, Hemmel racked up so many out-of-state trips away from Ida and the girls that by his account, their childhood just flew. He didn't bring home jewelry, sweets or anything dainty. He'd return from two weeks and two states away with a haul of collectible furniture —claw-footed tables, glass-front cabinets, ladder-back chairs, even a little walnut birthing stool, stark and angular. It looked like a hat rack for elves. Any piece of furniture that fit in the back seat of the Pontiac was fair game for Hemmel. Ida just learned to make room.

The living room held an uncomfortable loveseat of dark brown brocade, a tufted sofa in fading green floral with three buttons popped, a birchwood lamp table with pineapple curlicues on the corners, and a hand-carved mahogany coffee table, jungle-themed, the top embossed with crested parrots and bare-toothed tigers, its legs like elephant feet, thick and round, with toenails irregular as river rock. Nothing matched. It had never mattered to Hemmel and, over time, it didn't matter to her. They were just furnishings. She could relate.

Ida settled in her chair beside the window, opened the ring-bound notebook and folded it back on itself. She wrote a title at the top: Things in the World a Girl Needs to Know. Her pen paused there a long while. I'm a little rusty, she thought. She spent some time, then, studying the world of late summer in her unkempt lawn outside and a helpful truism finally occurred to her.

Eat the smallest dandelion greens; the big ones taste like turpentine.

That's a good start, she thought, and fell asleep in the chair until Jean Marie came through the door with a little melamine bowl of potato salad her mother had made but with no recorder. She said Joey Roneska was using it for dirty stuff so she had to use her mother's cell phone.

Ida was uneasy. "No pictures."

Jean Marie held up the little gadget. "Start now."

Her granddaughter reared back on her heels, aiming the eye of the phone. She was not listing anymore. Ida put up both hands.

"Start by saying your name."

"Ida Ellen Munzer." It came out more strongly than she expected. "I was a Strakel. My maiden name was Strakel."

"How old are you?"

"Seventy-three and a half."

"What do I need to know to be a person of good character in the world of tomorrow?"

"First thing, don't hijack an old lady's peaceful morning and make us cough up the secrets of life without some direction here."

Jean-Marie didn't budge. "Start with the A's."

"Always have a dollar in your shoe for the bus because every girl needs more than one way to get home."

"That's not an A. That's D, for dollar."

"Act like you don't care what people say about you. It'll drive them crazy."

"Grammy." Jean Marie whined like the teenager she was. "Those aren't very good. Tell me important things, wise things. Nice little sayings everyone knows."

"I'm not everyone, if you hadn't noticed. I'm not even anyone. Why are you asking me?"

"Because you're always telling people what to do."

"Then let me tell you and that little do-hickey of yours something, free of charge. I am a poor old woman with the flu in First Kings, West Virginia, and I have to talk into a gadget here because my granddaughter has got this impulse to put on airs for people and I got to stop it. I don't have a fancy bone in my body. Fancy don't give your kids no dinner, your car no gas, your landlord no rent. It don't give you no peace in marriage, either. Never won me no good will from my husband, a plain, hard man who I cannot imagine resting in peace. Bet he's looking up and down the beautiful walls of heaven every day to find cracks in the dry wall to complain about. If he's there. Gabriel might've had a look at his woebegone record and sent him right to hell."

"You can't say the h-word on a recording."

"Old folks say what they want. It's the consolation prize. We get the right to an angry heart and honest mouth because the longer we live, the more crap we have to take."

Jean Marie yanked the phone down. "My God, you almost said the s-word. You're messing me up. Mom said you would."

"She should be telling you more than that. Like how I earned my keep raising two kids, stretching every dime until it gave a quarter. Mealy mush dinners in the winter when the paycheck didn't come, mealy mush in the good times when he was working. Your granddad could not bring a paycheck straight home. Too many detours."

"All I remember is that Granddad was more fun than you. He laughed a lot when he drank. And he gave out quarters."

"What do you know about men and why they give out quarters? You're fourteen years old and worried about popping pimples on your nose and raising those little rose buds on your chest. That's all girls your age really worry about. This other stuff, wisdom from your elders, all that is fancy ideas from your school. It's not your own.

"It is, too, mine. I get to choose the people I interview. I get to ask them anything I want."

"Who else you got talking into the phone?"

"Mimi."

"You're getting maxims from that woman?"

"She lives right next door to you. It makes sense."

"You're recording that woman whose name I do not speak because she's Dex's mom and that's all she can ever be to me."

"Grammy, he's my dad. Stop piling up on him."

"It's not a pile up. It's keeping a promise. I promised that man no peace for coming on to my shy little Perty, just graduated secretarial school and working for the judge, a man of means. And here come Dex again, turns her heart soft as farmer's cheese and runs off with it, marries her, limpy-eyed, right in front of the judge she worked for. I would not, could not, go to the wedding."

"Then how'd you know she was limpy-eyed?"

"Mothers have their sources. That's a maxim for you: Make nice with the cashier at the Shop-a-Lot because she checks out everyone. She'll know more about your kin than you do."

"You should be happy they got married. That's how you got me, Bucky and Diane for grandkids."

"Yes, I did, but that was only half-due to Dex, let me remind you. I'm not a mean woman. I give that man some smiles across the years, mostly because you kids needed me to. Otherwise, I don't care to look in his direction or ask for his help."

"Mothers have their sources. That's a maxim for you: Make nice with the cashier at the Shop-a-Lot because she checks out everyone.

"Then who was it fixed your toilet and laid new pipe?" Jean Marie pointed outside. "Who ran electric to your shed and fixed the rotten wood in the porch? Daddy's a better man that you give him credit for. He's a better man than Granddad. Daddy doesn't drink up his paycheck."

"I don't talk to snotty kids."

"Mimi does. And she doesn't call me names."

"To your face."

"Mama said you'd turn mean on me if you found out about me recording Mimi."

"Mimi's not a respectable name for a grandmother. It's French, for little people. Her name's Bernice, plain old Bernice."

"Please, Grammy. Think about it. Write down your maxims. Then you can read them out loud to me. That'll work. I'll give you one more day, one more chance."

"What makes you think I want one?"

"Because I want it. It's for me. I want sayings from both grandmothers. Pretend we're a family for once before you die."

Before I die? "You're a few rungs short of a ladder, there, girl. How'd you jump from the flu to a headstone?"

"It's easy." Jean Marie packed the phone in her pocket. "You're slipping."

Ida was still working up a proper umbrage when Jean Marie turned and left the house. The hurt and huffiness was stuck inside with nowhere to go and Ida felt the build-up of a weight as dense as a bowling ball lurch up in her chest and roll her forward over her knees. She pulled herself up out of the chair. *Slipping?* She could not stop walking around the kitchen table, holding onto the top rungs of chairs, until she realized she was climbing a circle.

Her favorite granddaughter had gone to the Other Grandmother for what she needed. I'm not enough. Ida felt that she had been cut to half-full in the know-it-all department, at least in the eyes of Jean Marie. The slyness of it ticked her off. More irritating, Ida could not stand the idea that Dex's mom might have better advice than she herself. Jean Marie was using this as a love test. Making Ida compete with a woman she hated when, every visit, Ida showed that girl love, teasing her, insulting her dad, gigging her about her hard-headed mom, Ida's very own child, just to make her stronger. That was the goal of love. To make a child survive, make a mother stay, make a husband come home.

Ida knew about love tests. She had lived one her whole life. And she would not give up one jot of Jean Marie's love. If she had to fight for it, she'd fight, even face to face, with that old biddy. It was time to pay her neighbor a visit.

Ida flung aside the thin curtain that hung in the doorframe separating the kitchen from her small bedroom. Even in daytime there was barely enough light to see herself in the mirror on the vanity which occupied the darkest corner of the darkened room. Double-hung windows on each side of the bed were hidden by rubber-backed drapes that kept out heat and cold. In the mirror she was a shadowy shape. She preferred that. She used a few brisk strokes of a bristle brush to bunch her hair back. She put bobby pins in her teeth. Hands high behind her head, neck bent, she positioned a hair rat, a soft cigar of false hair, near the ends of the long strands in her hands. Her fingers tucked fast, rolling tight until all came together in a rolled arc at the nape of her neck. She pinned it securely. It was as much primping as she allowed herself.

Ida went out her back door and around to the side yard to get to the front yard. Use of a front door was only for show. The property line in the yard between her house and Bernice O'Brien's was unfenced and unmarked, except for the fact that Ida's grass was higher. Ida never crossed directly into Bernice's yard. She walked the line on her side of the grass until she reached the edge of the little paved road, turned left, walked fifteen yards and turned left again to face Bernice's house.

In its bones, it was like Ida's house and all the homes in Hoser Row, a latter-day vestige of company housing in a creek bottom in the little town of First Kings. The community had cropped up in boom time along the railroad line between two portals when coal was king. Frackers and gas rigs acted like road royalty these days, barely braking for two big S-curves through town. Ida's house, like Bernice's, had been built settlement style in a shotgun frame. One main hallway connected two mirrored living spaces, each with a kitchen and bedroom on the ground floor and two bedrooms upstairs. The east-facing window upstairs in Ida's house looked across at the west-facing window of the O'Brien's and that, in the case of Perty and Dex, had been that.

Ida stood on a swept path of neat concrete squares seated straight, kept even. She stared at Bernice's white porch posts, counted three pots of green ivy and dared a long brass wind chime to make a peep. A breeze surged. The brass tubes tingled with a happy sound that made Ida's soul twitch toward hate. The homewrecker. Now she was after Jean Marie with her maxims. Hemmel's unfaithfulness, Ida could live with. He was stone cold gone. She was used to that. Her granddaughter, living, learning and listing, was someone she could not live without.

Ida didn't even have to knock. There was Bernice's pale face peering through the front window with her small eyes and a smile that lifted her cheeks only as high as the powdered bags under her eyes. A second later, Bernice opened the door. "Been a while," she said.

"Nine years." Ida shrugged. "More or less."

"More. Come in."

"I'm busy," Ida said, standing in the foyer, looking straight ahead. "I won't take long."

"Sit down for a minute."

Bernice led her into the sitting room, an ornate array of filmy curtains, gold rope tie-backs, and ivory wallpaper with pink roses the size of cabbages. The sofa had three homemade needlepoint pillows accenting fat cushions. Her furniture was formal and very different from Ida's, except for one piece. Ida turned her back so that she didn't have to look at it. "I'll stand," she said. "I just came over to make sure you know that I've got maxims for Jean Marie. Lots of them."

Bernice smiled in a way that seemed deeply weary. "I'm sure you do."

Ida tried not to sound worried. "How many did you give her?"

Bernice shook her head as if it was hard to remember. "Two, three, maybe. Please sit down for me, Ida. My knees hurt."

Ida sat gingerly in a wing-backed chair, keeping her back straight so as not to take comfort from Bernice's furniture. "You can get shots, you know," she told Bernice. "For the knee pain. I got one at the clinic last year. Hurt me so bad I told them to stop."

"I know."

"What are saying?"

"You hit the nurse. Carol at the Shop-a-Lot told me."

"I flailed. It was a natural reaction."

"Carol said you knocked out a bottom tooth."

"It was just a flail."

"People can get hurt when you do that."

Ida thought about that a minute, then she looked at the coffee table, Hemmel's ugly mahogany coffee table with tiger faces and elephant legs. "Well, I take a lot of hurt before I flail."

"That's true," Bernice said softly.

"How come you kept that coffee table Hemmel gave you?"

"Mostly because it's not like me to have something like that. It's an oddity. Why do you keep yours?

"It's like me, I guess. It doesn't match a thing around it. I don't go with anything, either."

"That's why Hemmel always went home to you. He couldn't fool you. The rest of us, we bored him."

"Don't you dare talk about Hemmel as if you knew him. As if you knew how to endure him, how make a life with him."

"I didn't know him at all, Ida. It was so long ago I don't even remember whether we had fun or not."

"Rum and Royal Crown Cola?"

Bernice nodded.

"His favorite." Ida leaned forward and adjusted a ruffled doily to cover a tiger face on the coffee table. "I hope you had a good time. You sure paid for it."

"Lost husband number three." Bernice's smile seemed to go way past her eyes. "Went right out the door. Dex didn't like him as a stepdad anyway."

Ida sat straighter. She looked at Bernice. "I never lost my husband, did I?"

Bernice blinked. "No, Ida, you didn't."

They sat a moment with only the ticking of a grandfather clock by the window to make comment.

"Until he died," Ida said. A long breath left her chest. She stood to leave. "That did it."

Bernice scooted herself to the edge of the cushion, placed an arm on the each rest of the chair and pulled forward with a

Ida leaned forward and adjusted a ruffled doily to cover a tiger face on the coffee table. "I hope you had a good time. You sure paid for it."

mighty look of oomph on her face until she stood upright on uncertain knees. "About your tax bill. I told Dex he should pay it, if you'd let him."

"I don't want his help. I cannot stand being in debt to him or anyone else."

"He and Perty are going to get both of our houses when we die. You should consider it more like he's paying you some rent while you're still here. That makes it his debt, not yours."

"You've got a devious way of thinking, Bernice O'Brien. My mind doesn't work that way."

"Then here's the truth. If you lose the house, you'll have to move in with Perty and Dex." That stopped Ida. "Is that what they're saying?"

"You're too sick to live in someone's shanty and too proud to go to a nursing home. Where else do you think you'll end up?"

"There's a possibility I could die first. That would help."

"Consider letting the kids pay the bill, Ida. If not for yourself, for Jean Marie. You're worrying her sick."

"You don't know that."

"She loves you like the Rock of Ages. *Why* is the question."

Ida deliberated a moment on her need for Jean Marie and her creed to be free of debt, and as she stepped into the hallway, she realized how uncomfortable she felt in a house where everything hung, stood or stayed in its place. She looked at the elephant leg coffee table and felt sorry for it. Hemmel's table could not be itself here.

"I'll consider that offer on the tax bill," Ida said. "There's a condition, though. You have to tell me the maxims you gave Jean Marie."

"Oh, for goodness sake. Here you go." Bernice pulled two of the elaborate needlepoint pillows off of her sofa and held them up. "The sayings are right in front of you."

Ida read the hand-needled words sewn in pink cross-points. "'Home is where the heart is.'"

"This is my favorite," Bernice said. "'Love is a many-splendored thing.'"

"Thank you, Bernice," Ida said. "I mean it." Ida realized that Jean Marie desperately needed her maxims.

She reached her own back door short of breath. It was such a strain talking to Bernice. She paused a minute to put the leftover morning's coffee in a saucepan to heat up. Gas was cheaper than using electric in the microwave. That was not a maxim. It was common knowledge.

She wanted to start with the A's, just like Jean Marie wanted. It was not easy but Ida kept at it. She had to skip some letters and began to flag at suppertime but rallied with a sandwich made of a bread heel folded over her last Vienna sausage and made it past the letter F. Her digestion was a mess but she made it all the way to T before nature called her for a reckoning of the Vienna sausage and other hasty choices.

Things in the World a Girl Needs to Know

A

Argument. Have one every day to keep your wits and your friends sharp.

B

Bit O' Honey. The best candy, bar none, but you'll need a dentist.

Barometric pressure. It's that outside-pushing-in feeling the air gets before bad weather. It's also the feeling you get before you hit a child or have a stroke. It's a warning. Respect it.

C

Crimea. Your grandfather's father came from a land on the edge of the Crimean Sea and stowed away after he crossed a desert full of crazy men on horses. That's all I know of the story but I want you to know we've got a desert in the family.

C-words. There are bad C-words out there. Ernest Hildebrand called me one once in high school. Never pretend you want something from a boy primed to give it to you.

D

Dad. I will not read this D into your gadget. Dex O'Brien is a daddy with a strong heart and fair mind. Your other grandmother raised a good husband for my Perty. Do not use my name.

E

Engagement ring. Don't waste your money. Get the clincher.

F

Furniture. It needs you to know two things: Lemon paste for oak pieces and olive oil for maple.

Fear. It comes in two sizes. Soft and jittery like a rabbit in the weeds, or hard and thundering like a buffalo in your chest. Rabbit-size is harder to take care of. It'll jitter you all the way to an early death.

G

Groundhog. Once he digs a tunnel, he'll drive you nuts, even if he's not there.

Grudge. Every woman needs a good, juicy, bitter one. It builds up the jaundice in hard times, gives you color. But mind the passing of time. You have to strike back early, before your grudge has progeny. Otherwise you got a mother on your hands. Be careful. See M.

H

Home-wrecker. A woman that has a habit of making a man momentarily feel unique. She could be saying, "We need paper in the outhouse," or, "Rain's coming in," and she looks on him with such full-faced attention, he can't hear straight and he thinks she said that he's the king of the sun, moon and stars, and what a manly package he is, and he treats her like a queen.

I

Innocence. Innocence is not bliss. It's just the blind side of the moon, waiting to turn.

K

Kittens. If you want to know how to play, watch a kitten chase a moth. It'll teach you how to make a toy out of thin air.

Keratin. A part of the body nobody respects but everybody cares about. It's that finishing touch. On a bird it's feathers and her bill. On a ram it's his fur and butting horn. On me, it's my nails, that's a hand-tool, you know, and my hair. That's the keratin that carries my heritage. I didn't draw much Cherokee out of my mother so I was left with this fine wisp her parents brought from Wales and the blondish curl from my dad. So make the most of what you got from your folks while you're young because it's only going to lean light and Scot-Irish when you get older, and I do mean lean.

L

Lies. Men tell these. Women, too. I lied when I told you Perty's potato salad needed pickles. One lie doesn't mark a person false. Twenty-three, though, is too much reinforcement of a bad thing. I'm getting close.

Lilies. These are a flower that makes anyone feel elegant. I don't have a sophisticated bone in my body, so when Hemmel handed me a lily bouquet on the first date, I took on airs I didn't deserve. I could've ruled a kingdom, until they died.

Love. It burns brighter for all the winds arrayed against it. Enjoy it until you get a northerly. Find an ember and don't lose it. Just hunker down.

Lugnut. Do not let the mechanic tighten yours too much.

M

Mothers. Don't get sappy about the job. It's only for the brave and the vigilant. The law of all mothers applies: Hurt me, fine. But don't you touch my kids.

N

Neighbor. The good book tells us to love thy neighbor as thyself, so don't be that fond of yourself. That cuts down the requirement right there.

P

Potato. You can fry it or throw it, whichever comes in handier.

Punctilious people. These are folks who appear to be severe when they're really just particular. Learn from how prissy and precise they are and how they follow a rule. The formalities can save your life someday. Strict people know the rules, where they bend and where they break. You need one punctilious friend. That's about all you can stand, anyway.

R

Regret. This is important. It's a place to visit, but not too long. It's in that dark corner of the far pantry filled with all we have lost. Open the door to get a whiff of the long gone. Then close it tight.

Rose. This is a good name for a child but it will not foreordain her to blossom like you want. Rose dropped out in tenth grade to party in Cincinnati with a friend and find work in the glass factory. Next thing we know she's making collars for men's shirts in a factory in Indianapolis. No marriage. No kids. No contact. Plenty of whiskey. Her name is still a blossom, though. Can't take that away.

Rucksack. Have one packed at all times with a pair of clean underwear, mad money and a spare key. You might want to let yourself back in.

T

Teaberry. This is a naturally odd flavor in a stick of gum and you've got to love it. It'll bring back memories of swiping a leaf off a tree and sucking a little trace of juice from the stem. I was going to name my firstborn son Teaberry for the flavor I loved and the plain sweet melody you can call out in such a name. I'm glad we went with Tom. Stillborn, anyway.

Time. Let this pass.

Ida smoothed a cramp in her writing hand. A dusky sky made it difficult to see the page and she could tell she was drifting between the lines. She felt done in. What else did she have to teach Jean Marie, anyhow?

The question didn't linger. Ida's ear caught rustling sounds in the far corner of the yard, the garden. Ida pulled herself up straight and leaned close to the screen of the open window. She saw a furry brown body amble from the doghouse to the bean patch, in no particular hurry.

Son of a gun.

Two smaller varmints popped heads out of the doghouse door, tested the air then followed their mother to the garden, stopping to tumble over each other and play-wrestle.

Think it's a party?

Ida saw the leaves of her potato plants lift and fall as the babies wriggled underneath. Ahead of them, a spray of black dirt arced out of the garden and hit the fence. When it stopped, the mother groundhog rose out of the patch, erect on two legs. In her paws was a potato, Ida's only respectable harvest of the season, claws cupped over each end of the spud like a squeezebox she knew how to play.

The groundhog's broad belly made a can't-miss target. Ida rose out of the rocker to reach her rifle propped in the corner. It took all of her strength to move with stealth and no sound Before she could grasp the gun, a hissing intake of back pain gave her away.

Mama Groundhog froze upright, eyes on the window.

Ida was surprised at her own panic. She seemed caught in a spotlight, her murderous intent exposed. Ida got one hand around the barrel and lifted quickly. The long rifle slipped out of her hand. Its nose slid straight down the corner of the wall and landed hard on the floor. The gun went off on impact.

The young groundhogs scrambled out of the garden in a leaping run for the doghouse. As the shot reverberated in the air, the mother groundhog remained upright, big and broad,

The long rifle slipped out of her hand. Its nose slid straight down the corner of the wall and landed hard on the floor.

facing the house. Her pups disappeared through the door of the doghouse, then she ducked in an instant and was gone.

Shaking, Ida fell back into the chair. She had not been hit but she would not be surprised if the village of mice that lived in the kitchen wall had all been struck dead of a heart attack. Bound to be a stench. She closed her eyes. The picture that came to mind was a tunnel. Mama groundhog and her pups wriggling safe and sound through a channel Ida could never close, poison or fill up.

"Ida!" The front door shook with a pounding. "Open up!"

It was nosy Bernice.

"Ida Ellen Munzer, if you didn't kill yourself, open the door this instant or I'm calling an ambulance and you'll have to pay for it."

Threats. Just like her. "Coming," Ida said, as loud as she could, which was not very, but the window was open. An old eavesdropper like Bernice would hear just fine.

Ida rose on unsteady legs and groped the wall.

"Ida!" Bernice pounded.

Coming. Ida reached the front door, breathing fast, shallow. She slipped the lock and placed both hands on the knob. The door hadn't been opened in years. She pulled. *Where's my strength?*

"Ida!" Bernice kept pounding.

Warped wood shuddered and cracked. Dried paint gave way and hinges squealed protest. The door finally swung free.

Ida leaned hard into the frame. She could barely hold herself upright.

Bernice crossed the threshold. "Are you shot?"

Ida shook her head, disbelieving. Bernice O'Brien. Traipsing right through the front door. Ida caught a breath. "Fumbled my gun."

"Silly woman," Bernice said, pulling Ida's arm around her neck and grasping her waist so that Ida could stand free of the wall. "Let's sit a bit."

Bernice and her bad knee got Ida and her wobbly legs to the sofa. They plopped down as one, bouncing inward against one another when the couch cushions sank low on broken springs. They straightened as best they could and sat, breathing hard.

Ida was petrified with embarrassment. She had a bullet hole in the wall, a splintered foot in the rocker, a home wrecker neighbor sitting an elbow jab away and Ida would have to thank her.

No question, I'm slipping.

Ida let that sink in and grew aware of a lively feeling across the top of her head. Her stingy grey hair was flitting and flopping in the breeze funneled through the opened door, gaping wider.

"Fresh air feels so good," Bernice said.

Ida ventured a real look at her neighbor. Thirty-five years of endless umbrage and nothing flitted out of place in that dark dyed helmet of hers. A deep question moved Ida.

"How much lacquer do you use on that hair-do?" she asked.

"Oh, for heaven's sake, Ida." Bernice reached a hand to each temple, loosened and lifted. The wig slipped into her hand like a well-fed pet. "You're welcome."

That's how Jean Marie found them. ■

RIVALRY

For our mother

Oooh—that bad seaside vacation you spent
Caught in the surf of my warring sisters
(That they were engaged or married was no matter)—
I saw you felt again how selfishly we fought

For your regard, your very eye,
Should you turn to exclaim or reply,

Or even back when you read to us, a group
Of four, your eyes lowered to the book,
With Susan, littlest, in your lap;
Mike, aloof, but touching you with his foot;
And Cathy, jockeying your elbow, who is like
You, perhaps . . .
                                        Even I watched, your distant hawk,
For your wink that meant to me, your oldest—this story
And jealousy, after all, would be beneath me.

MARY JANE WHITE

FORSYTHIA

1
Shallow spring & the great act fails
The forsythia freezes
A half-dozen buds on each of several stems
Which for them means a weak few
& then summer
& likely leaves crimped to the red stems
Which then will spread

2
Sunlight & eventually
A white-blue bold jay will come here jumping
Dividing the right claw from the left
Shaking everything then rustling busily
Settling his wings

3
Which may allow your glance
No more
To pass over this
No more than a simple thoughtlessness
That opens endlessly
One of several inanities

4
One mistake is that you forget
You think you can go everywhere
In essence

5
As presentiments of every far-off moment
Your wings close
You dive on the far side of the moon in the dust
Blind to your sweepings

6
In the dry grey dust
Where you are still bathing
& beaking about to find whether the forsythia's
Fallen buds are perhaps still edible

7
But the joy of you is
That of unforced coupling
As when you knew only impersonal hatred
Which then was the only thinkable sort

8
& you remain oblivious of any fence
However high it might be
While intimation seems to run so certainly
As if upon unblistered feet
Painlessly

9
& nowhere does the gate within open

10
But there are knitted strings
& straw perched in the eaves
& birdcalls from before you were born
When everything was a waking woman
& a blessing spoken

11
& then the opening after
& the man & woman were turned out

12
Still they are still here
Out in one of the fields
A field with an open gate
Dull & shadowed by low clouds

13
& the gate is forgotten in its own rejoicing

14
For our rootedness began in this dull field
Where we were rows upon rows
& where we did multiply
& there is nothing to be done
With any account of us

15
& the essence outside us grows still
& there is no guilty feeling

16
It is coming to its end here

17
The familiar shrinking of the creek in summer
& the silence of the perching jay
As it sits quietly going nowhere in the heat

18
That heat & how you will become uncertain you know
    anything
The watery dull stream & the plucked corpse on its bank
The dust & how you stared at it again
From one level of your adult stature
& the blood dried newly brown
With no way to change this
The armies of streaming ants
The drill and business then in the jay's heart
As it lay before you
As once the silence of a single woman spread
Without price

19
The silence of the jay sinking thinning flattening
To a papery essence
Blindly lifted at one edge by the wind

20
You will have forgotten you found anything in this field
& the forsythia is both red & green
& yellow

21
& the light of the moon is reflected

MARY JANE WHITE

SUMMER: WITH A MAGNET

We dredged the roadside dust
For iron filings, for hours.
Fringe to a blackened finger.

The boy next door drank kitchen cleaner
And had to have his stomach pumped.
This happened also to each of us—once.

I ate Drano.
Cathy—aspirin—a bottle's worth.
On the screened-in porch, baby Susan

Was bitten through her baby finger by a beetle.
We battled with wet brooms against the wasps.
I wouldn't die when Michael broke my vein.

Trains whistled by. The vapor trails
Of planes crossed the sky and one another.
The storms swept over.

MARY JANE WHITE

MAGICAL REALISM WITH AN AUTHENTIC VOICE

REBECCA D. ELSWICK

My love of magical realism has been part of my reading and writing life long before I knew the genre had a name. When I was a little girl, I used to sit on a stool in my grandmother's kitchen and watch her cook. While she chopped, stirred, and made the best biscuits in the world, she would tell stories about ghosts—*haints,* she called them.

The story I recall most vividly was about a woman who died of a broken heart, searching for her young son, who had been stolen by Native Americans. According to Granny, the woman and her child were "black Irish," which meant they had coal-black hair and dark brown eyes. One morning, when the woman left the boy asleep in their cabin and went out to look for food, the Indians came and stole the child because they thought he looked like them. It was winter, and the poor woman walked through the woods day after day, crying and searching for her child until she grew ill and died. Granny said that she believed the woman really died from a broken heart.

This was the point in the story when my granny would take my hand and lead me to the back porch that faced the woods. She would point at the distance and say, "To this day, her haint walks these woods looking for her boy. If you go too far into the forest you can hear her crying, and you just might see her haint." Then Granny would disappear back into the kitchen and leave me staring into the trees. Needless to say, this kept me from ever wandering too far from the house, which was no doubt Granny's reason for telling the story in the first place. What she didn't know was that she was instilling in me a love of stories and storytelling, especially about haints. As I grew to love and study many literary genres, I never forgot my grandmother's stories of haints and magic that lived side-by-side with her homemade biscuits and backyard garden. These stories were, I discovered, steeped in magical realism, a multinational term that has a complex and rich history.

Magical realism was first used by Franz Roh in 1925 to describe German post-expressionist painting. Two years later, it was applied to literature by Italian novelist Massimo Bontempelli, but it was largely forgotten until 1940 when the term *lo real maravilloso*, or "marvelous realism," was resurrected to describe postcolonial Latin American literature.

In 1955, magical realism was used by Angel Flores in his essay "Magical Realism in Spanish American Fiction," in which he contends that the genre has its roots in the romantic realism of Spanish-language literature.[1]

Magical realism is a serious branch of fiction that focuses on ordinary people going about the everyday activities of life in a real-world setting. Everything is normal except for one or two fantastical elements that go beyond the realm of possibility. Whether it be magic or fate, or a physical connection with the earth and her creatures, magical realism must celebrate the ordinary.

In Maggie Ann Bowers's book *Magic(al) Realism*, she says, "One of the unique features of magical realism is its reliance upon the reader to follow the example of the narrator in accepting both realistic and magical perspectives of reality on the same level. It relies upon the full acceptance of the veracity of the fiction during the reading experience, no matter how different this perspective may be to the reader's nonreading opinions and judgements."[2] This gets to the heart of what I am exploring: how does a writer create a believable world with magical elements that the reader will accept? And one step further: how does an Appalachian writer create believable magical elements based on folklore, such as the Scots-Irish folklore steeped in ancestry?

Stories with magical realism can reasonably take place in any real-world locale, but many of them are set in small towns and rural areas. One reason that these stories frequently take place in less populated areas is that magical realism often involves nature or the natural world, whether that be in the

1 Erik Camayd-Freixas. "Reflections on Magical Realism: A Return to Legitimacy, the Legitimacy of Return." http://dll.fiu.edu/people/faculty/erik-camayd-freixas/reflections_on_magical_realism.pdf

2 Maggie Ann Bowers. *Magic(al) Realism* (Abingdon: Routledge, 2004), 4.

woods out behind the characters' houses or the ocean down the path from their front porch. In *Magic(al) Realism*, Bowers says, "It has been noted that magical realist fiction are often set in rural areas away from the influence over, or influence from, the political power centers."[3]

This observation certainly applies to Appalachian literature, in which many books are rich in Native American and European folklore. Two such works—*Ghost Riders* by Sharyn McCrumb and *Bloodroot* by Amy Greene—brim with magical elements: ghosts and spirits; nonlinear time; history; and invisible forces like enchanted objects, dreams, myths, and legends which are elements that appear time and again in magical realism. The people and the cultures described in

The people and cultures described in these books makes the reader respect the magic…It often opens the readers' eyes to the ills of their cultural past in a way they've never seen it before.

these books makes the reader respect the magic, altering their conventional view of reality, which is the goal of the writer of magical realism. It often opens the readers' eyes to the ills of their cultural past in a way they have never seen it before.

Ghost Riders is a novel with the magical elements of ghosts, spirits, and legends that examines the Civil War. The focus of the novel is the hatred between the white mountain people who were forced to choose sides, Confederate or Union. According to Andrea Garrett in *The Greenman Review*, "One of the themes of the novel is that hate doesn't die just because the incident that caused it is over. In *Ghost Riders*, the long-lasting hatred of the war in the mountains is causing a rift in the fabric of time in which the past (those who actually fought in the war) and the present (the reenactors who are reliving this past time for whatever reason) are swirling together. This rift cannot be mended without a blood price."[4]

The rift in time in *Ghost Riders* is an example of how magical realists use nonlinear time in their stories. Bruce Holland Rogers writes in "Get Unreal: Expressionism, Surrealism, Magical Realism, and Fantasy" that "Time does not always march forward in the magical realist world view. The distant past is present in every moment, and the future has already happened. Great shifts in the narrative's time sequence reflect a reality that is almost outside of time. This accounts for ghosts, premonitions, and the feeling that time is a great repetition rather than a progression."[5]

In *Ghost Riders*, McCrumb writes about three Civil War era characters, Zebulon Baird Vance, McKesson (Keith) and Malinda Blalock. She records historically accurate stories of Malinda, a woman who dressed as a male soldier to fight alongside her husband, Keith, and the famous governor of North Carolina (Zebulon Vance), to provide a frame of realistic reference that enhances credibility. In the present day of the novel, Civil War reenactors recreate a famous battle. Then, McCrumb creates Civil War soldiers to slip through a rift in time and show up in modern day. These soldiers are ghosts that manifest in modern day because McCrumb borrows the belief of a world where some people can be "betwixt and between" this world and the next from Scottish folklore.[6]

3 Ibid., 32.

4 Andrea S. Garrett. "Sharyn McCrumb, Ghost Riders." http://thegreenmanreview.com/gmr/book/book_mccrumb_ghostriders.html

5 Bruce Holland Rogers. "Get Unreal: Expressionism, Surrealism, Magical Realism, and Fantasy." *Flash Fiction Online.* January 2009. http://www.flashfictiononline.com/c20090102-get-unreal-expressionism-surrealism-magical-realism-fantasy-bruce-holland-rogers.html

6 Sharyn McCrumb. *Ghost Riders* (New York: Dutton, 2003).

In a Civil War reenactment scene of *Ghost Riders*, a Confederate soldier appears at the camp. He is thin and bedraggled, but dressed in such authentic garb that the reenactors stare at him. He asks for directions to his battalion in a thick mountain accent. When one of the reenactors gives him directions, he disappears down the road, but none of the men, who should have encountered him on their way, saw him. These ghosts, especially the band of spirits that appear on horseback, begin appearing to people in the mountains of western North Carolina when the Civil War reenactors restage a violent piece of Southern history.

McCrumb's ghost riders are drawn from a mountain legend that says a band of ghosts on horseback roam the mountains of western North Carolina and east Tennessee. In life, they were renegade Union sympathizers who plundered and murdered their way across the mountains during the war. In her book *Sharyn McCrumb's Appalachia*, McCrumb writes, "The mountain conflict was not the Civil War in the *Gone with the Wind* sense, but much more the sense of Afghanistan or Bosnia. It was a terrible, terrible time."[7]

To repair this rift in time, McCrumb creates the characters Rattler and Nora Bonesteel. Rattler and Nora both have the "sight" and are the key to the novel's magical elements. Rattler is a healer who can see spirits. Nora Bonesteel can see the future. Rattler and Nora walk "betwixt and between" this world and the next, so they understand what is happening when ghosts begin to appear. Both characters use their gifts to close this portal that allows the past to infringe upon the present.

McCrumb's use of the sight in *Ghost Riders* is taken from Scots-Irish folklore to create a believable but fantastical landscape. In Elizabeth Sutherland's *Ravens and Black Rain*, she records the story of the Highland second sight through the centuries. She says, "Here are some of the ingredients of what has come to be recognized as traditional Highland sight: spontaneous unsought vision; the precognition of impending disaster; the physical changes that affect the seer; the prophecy that looks to the far future."[8]

Magical realism, when used fittingly, adds layers and depth to the story. This is especially true in Amy Greene's novel *Bloodroot*. Bloodroot is an actual plant which has a red blood-like sap used both as medicine and poison. In the book *Bloodroot*, it is the name of the mountain—the setting for Greene's story that she lovingly describes with its luscious woods, winding hollows, and streams filled with blue gill. Bloodroot Mountain sets the scene for a story of healing and magic juxtaposed with a story of mothers and their children and generations of violence. Greene paints a portrait of a natural wonderland with the plant bloodroot functioning as a symbol of healing and harming. Actual blood works in similar ways in the novel, as family connections both heal and harm the characters.[9]

The book is told in many voices and spans from the Great Depression to today. Women form the focus of the novel: the matriarch Byrdie, her daughter Clio, her granddaughter Myra, and Myra's daughter, Laura. The parallels between these generations of women are not just their magical abilities, but their ability to fall in love with unsavory men.

Byrdie's magical gift is "the touch"—a sort of ESP. Byrdie's grandmother, Ruth, had the magical ability to let her spirit leave her body:

7 Sharyn McCrumb. *Sharyn McCrumb's Appalachia* (Nashville: Oconee Spirit Press, 2011), 42.

8 Elizabeth Sutherland. *Ravens and Black Rain: The Story of Highland Second Sight* (New York: Corgi Books, 1987), 17.

9 Amy Greene. Bloodroot (New York: Knopf, 2009).

> *Grandma had the best gift of all. She claimed she could send her spirit up out of her body. She said, "You could lock me up in the jailhouse or bury me alive down under the ground. It don't matter where this old shell is at. My soul will fly off wherever I want to be." She told me about the time she fell down in a sinkhole when she was little and couldn't climb back out... She looked up at the sun between the roots hanging down like dirty hair and wished so hard to fly up out of there that her spirit took off, rose, and soared on back to her little house in the holler. That's when she figured out what her gift was.*[10]

Greene uses a variety of rich imagery to concoct a world of magical realism tied to the landscape. In an interview, Greene said, "Much of the magical elements in *Bloodroot* come from my childhood—from stories passed down orally. I also did research on the subject and learned a great deal studying folk healing at Vermont College."[11] Among those elements are the colors: blue, black and red; mountain superstitions, a wild mare named Rose, a simple hand-carved wooden box, and most prominent, the power of the plant bloodroot. Besides the red sap of bloodroot, Greene uses the color black to describe the rich earth on Bloodroot Mountain and John Odom who looks "almost foreign, hair and eyes black as soot."[12]

Blue is used to describe Myra's eyes—"haint blue". It is also important in portraying Bloodroot Mountain as a place where magic is a common occurrence, as often as a bird flies across the blue sky. According to Byrdie, haint blue is a special color that wards off evil spirits *Ravens and Black Rain, Ravens and Black Rain,* with haint blue eyes, Byrdie hopes the curse that was put on her family by their spiteful Aunt Della, will finally end. When the curse was pronounced, Della said it could not be lifted until there was a baby born in their line with haint blue eyes. Byrdie told Myra that as soon as Della cursed them, terrible things started happening. As Byrdie described it, "That old devil knows ain't nobody been born with blue eyes in our family for generations."[13]

Like other magical realist novels, the natural world is key. In *Bloodroot,* nature is central to the identity of Byrdie—her mother, grandmother and sisters, and Myra. Bloodroot Mountain, the actual bloodroot plant, and the horse Rose, who refuses to be tamed, play a large part in the family's vision of the world and in their magical relationship to it. But despite their magical gifts, this novel is also about a poverty-stricken family surrounded by violence. At its end, *Bloodroot* arrives at a resolution of sorts—not unlike life itself. This Appalachian tale leaves us with a wisp of peace, arms full of forgiveness, and the knowledge that another generation is about to tangle, hopefully, with the future.

This Appalachian tale leaves us with a wisp of peace, arms full of forgiveness, and the knowledge that another generation is about to tangle, hopefully, with the future.

Greene subtlety weaves magical elements into the story, accentuating the elements of magical realism. The magic is present in these women, but it does not "save" them from their fate. Superstitious Appalachian folklore, like painting a door "haint blue" to ward off evil, and the belief that a child who gets the "thresh" can be cured by the breath of a man who

10 Ibid., 7.
11 Amy Greene, Personal Interview, Telephone, 1 February 2017.
12 Greene, *Bloodroot,* 49.
13 Ibid., 9.

has never seen his father, are from Scots-Irish lore. When the child, Byrdie gets the thresh, the women take her to Clifford Pinkston's farm where they find him outside working. All Byrdie's mother says is, "This'n here's got the thresh...I was hoping we could trouble you to help us out." And Clifford gets down on his knees, puts his mouth over Byrdie's, and blows his breath into her lungs. "I could feel my lungs filling up with it. It was such a relief someway that I wanted to squall. He pulled back from me, still holding my face, and we looked for a while in each other's eyes. It seemed like even the birds in the trees had quit making noise."[14]

Bloodroot has all the elements of magical realism. Myra's character is the link between five generations that loop forward and backward in time. She ties magical elements to the landscape to create rich imagery, but the characters are real people struggling to survive poverty and harsh living conditions.

All fiction is essentially a game of make-believe in which the author conceives characters and situations and sets them down on paper. But the writer of magical realism must make the reader accept her premise of a strange and marvelous world, while inducing the reader to suspend disbelief. Yet while the techniques of magical realism might at first look something like fantasy, the form is trying to do more than play with reality's rules. It is conveying realities that other people really do experience, or once experienced.

Gabriel Garcia Marquez—famous for his use of magical realism in such novels as *Love in the Time of Cholera*—was asked by the *New York Times*, after winning the Nobel Prize in Literature, about the origin of his magical realist writing. He said, "Grandfather was a former colonel who told endless stories of the civil war of his youth, took me to the circus and the cinema and was my umbilical cord with history and reality.

Grandmother was always telling fables, family legends and organizing our life according to the messages she received in her dreams. She was the source of the magical, superstitious and supernatural view of reality."[15]

Like Marquez traced his magical writing to his grandparents' stories, I believe that much of the magical realism present in Appalachian literature comes from folklore and stories gathered from family and friends. In my own work, I have studied how these authors create worlds rich with magical elements drawn from history. I have read legends and myths, probed dreams and reveled in ghosts and spirits. I have followed time through loops of present to past and onward to the future. Most of all, I have explored how magical realist authors explore a country's culture and folklore in their stories to create a believable alternate reality. In the words of Sharyn McCrumb, "in Appalachia the magic is already here." ■

14 Ibid., 22.

15 Simons, Marlise. "A Talk with Gabriel Garcia Marquez." *The New York Times*. http://www.nytimes.com/books/97/06/15/reviews/marquez-talk.html. 1982.

GOD AS EDIE
THE KNOXVILLE ZOO ELEPHANT WHO CRUSHED AND KILLED HER KEEPER, STEPHANIE JAMES, 14 JANUARY 2011

They had to believe she knew not what she'd done.

Pent up, spent of a thousand, thousand wasted days,
though, maybe she meant that murderous misbehavior,
the one myopic tragic move left in her DNA,
no longer able to judge
distances or love.

In the colonnade of her bones a stampede
had waited for the trunk of her to swing,
perhaps, her tusk a wish to brush a human clavicle,
let go the cavalcade of snorts
her trunk in exhortation held back
every other time before just like a blessing.

The lively blithe blonde lifted upward
her final gift, an offering of communion toward
the open grey-pink, wrinkled mouth
a precious snack, unwitting sacrifice,
without a breath of hesitation at the evening's altar.

There is no way to punish this calamity:

The keeper's lovely body fell, it falls, it is falling,
the memory of the falling held above all else,

a plodding memory capable of holding every equal sorrow
inside that tree-bark skin and lumbering bone and blood,
inside the mind inside that massive drudgery of skull.

SUSAN O'DELL UNDERWOOD

SWALLOW FALLS

It took some climbing to perch on that rock above the rapids
surrounded by sound, the roaring magnified among mountains
in a stillness of green-black spruce.

I crawl to the edge, belly on sandstone, stare twenty feet down
to a pool, a miracle of disappearance and darkness and depth
with white water seething around.

I study the falls while you catch the day's only fish, a small sunny,
unlock the barb from the soft bone jaw, let it fall to the pool
with a plink. The surface heals over the sound.

Boulders surround us, totems shaped by an ancient sea then left
a moment. One day they'll dislodge and wash from these shoals
into an age of peace.

Above the far slope, a beam of sun in a haze of campfire smoke.
I've lain on this boulder long enough, feeling how small a man can be,
an anxious man among deafening waters.

As we hike back the uphill trail, I get winded, stop to rest on a fallen tree,
then coax myself on through needles and leaves. We climb from the forest
and catch the heartrending call.

Two hikers are coming behind us, and before they emerge from the trailhead,
we know what they're crying for. The shape and feel of each word
breaks over the sound of the falls.

DAVID SALNER

CHAFF

Sunlight floods the loft, barn chaff explodes
into the summer heat, a sparkling vapor
spirals into roof-beam shadows. A day's work
dazzles, won't settle, floats upward, a flood of particles
glittering in the August sun. A moment of silence
transfixed by dust.

Seated on the floor, back against rough planks,
sweat-soaked, skin itchy with hay—if I still smoked
I'd pass a crush-proof pack to you, and we'd exhale the
 dust
and watch it circle toward a dying sun. The two of us.

DAVID SALNER

RESIGNATION

This world is not puréed, but for you
I make it so. Every day a blender grinds
raw morning smooth against the chance
you will disgorge food barely chewed.

When I was young you forced the spoon,
such rough devotion to nourish, to school
the stubborn in me. Now I mother
produce to appease. The texture

your life wants, I cannot tender,
though I wish it could be. Dementia
has choked you out of speech,
your memory, a raging fist.
What kindness can, let me blend
with anger, carrot, banana, fear.

JANE MILLER

RECKONING

The coffin where I keep my dead words
is open. The jewelry box, pink like young skin,
where I store trinkets is shut. The ballerina

inside her pink tutu face down
on her footed spring, waits for the hand
that opens her. She must be tired, always rising

over the horizon of my face. Outside, an egret stands
in the marsh, a white flag marking my surrender
to the wind. On my walls, swallows painted

in their frames are gone. Where worms
will crawl, they peck at my casket words, beaks
typing on pine, fresh-cut unlined. In bed,

I am a ghost form breathing ruffles
into sheets pulled taut as paper,
my wallpaper wilting like corsages

that once romanced my wrist, my shoulder
where babies clung. On the blanket stand,
my burial dress, all scattered florals.

I will be nosegay, cabbage head
with blue hydrangea perm,
my eyes' fringed curtains finally

closed, my nose never more
to be unstuffed, and my mouth,
with helpful stitching, seamed shut.

Where are my babies now?

I have seen enough bodies
to know how rouge helps death
blush. I hope the satin words comfort me,
that the birds leave enough.

JANE MILLER

BOOK REVIEW

Laura Leigh Morris. *Jaws of Life*. Morgantown, W.Va.: Vandalia Press, 2018. 168 pages. Softcover. $18.99.

Reviewed by Emily Masters

Laura Leigh Morris's debut collection of short stories, *Jaws of Life*, focuses on characters from a small town in West Virginia. Morris, who has had her fiction published in *The Louisville Review*, *Weave Magazine*, and other journals, gathers together some gems from previous publications alongside never before seen short stories that are guaranteed to strike a chord in the hearts of readers. The collection features sixteen of Morris's short stories centered on West Virginians from all walks of life and full of trouble.

While the characters in Morris's stories are not directly linked, they all share in common the small town of Brickton,

West Virginia, around which Morris paints a vivid sense of place. Her use of dialect deepens the culture of the place she conjures, and her scenes are fully developed. The coal site in "Frackers," the local tire shop in competition with the chain tire store in "House of Tires," the dingy local diner in "Fat Bottomed Girls" that serves greasy food and a good time, and the country fairgrounds in "Popular" all serve to signal Appalachia at every turn.

Themes including fracking, high school football, community, religion, and poverty, will be familiar to anyone who has a relationship to the Appalachian region. Morris thus ensures that readers see Appalachia in a current light. She includes an example of grassroots activism against a fracking company, a gay character who struggles with his identity in his community, and highlights Appalachia as a place with access to technology.

Such characters in these stories are clearly part of the modern world. The one exception is the old man in "Grief" who replaces his wife with a dog, even dressing the dog in his wife's clothing. Although the character's deep grief explains his bizarre behavior, the man's deviant sexuality reads a little too much like the stereotype of Appalachians as somehow less than human. Morris does, however, make sure to show this elderly character is not the norm.

Perhaps most importantly, Morris weaves in historical context that helps to explain the behavior of her characters. No situation in her stories is without explanation, and while none of her characters are saints (thankfully), their actions are real. Her characters make mistakes and have to pick their battles, both internal and external.

From outside-the-region bullies Ernie and Oscar, with their mock-country style in "Brickton Boys"; to Ruth, the frazzled single mother in "Winners"; to Everett and Bradley, who are struggling with their sexuality in "The Dance"; Morris's characters ring true.

Morris should be commended for the diversity of her characters. She manages to give them vitality in such few pages whether that character is a teenage girl struggling with the trials of a changing body, a woman in a knitting circle at prison, or a young man who is a master of funeral photography. Although the longest story in *Jaws of Life* is only sixteen pages long, her characters are fully realized.

Each story in this collection is standalone and bite-sized. But readers will be left looking forward to their next chance to sit down with Morris's writing. Her stories are exciting, full of twists, of mistakes, and of the uncertainty about where one decision can take a character. It is this balance that makes *Jaws of Life* so satisfying. These stories feel like real life instead of just words on a page. ■

ARS POETICA, APPA-LATCH-UH

Voices huddled along waters' edges
singing lines panegyric of rolling hills,
God, and granny witches. They praised
her feeble hands, patchwork quilts, myths
about godless souls, machines, but their
prudence did not stop the dig or the fear
of coal dust in our mouths. Now we pine
for those lost landscapes, immortalize
romantic turns of phrases, sell imitation
granny-quilts at retail price,
but those, those were *their* days,
their thoughts and their ways.

How do we build *this* time,
write our tales, replant our thyme?
With a little more acid to taste
the mud where coyotes roam
instead of red wolves, their bones arcane
in red clay along those deified waters' edges.
With resurrections of blackbirds
they shot for kicks, so silence will erupt
under lakes of drowned history,
the void necessary to let our skins speak,
tongues bite, climaxes reach, tradition sink.

KELSEY A. SOLOMON

CONTRIBUTORS

Bryce Berkowitz is an MFA candidate at West Virginia University. He is the Editor-in-Chief at *Cheat River Review*. His work has appeared or is forthcoming in *Best New Poets 2017, Ninth Letter, Third Coast, Passages North, The Pinch, Hobart, Barrow Street, Permafrost, Eleven Eleven, Tampa Review, Hawai'i Pacific Review, The Laurel Review,* and *The Fourth River,* among other publications.

Hal Crowther is an award-winning critic, essayist, and journalist whose work has appeared in *Time, Newsweek, Oxford American, Granta,* and *Narrative* magazines. He is the author of four essay collections and *An Infuriating American: The Incendiary Arts of H.L. Mencken*. His third essay collection, *Gather at the River,* was a finalist for the National Book Critics Circle prize for criticism. He lives in Hillsborough, North Carolina, with his wife, novelist Lee Smith.

Rebecca D. Elswick is the daughter and granddaughter of coal miners, and lives in southwestern Virginia. *Mama's Shoes,* her debut novel, was published in 2011, and *No Stopping Her,* her first young adult novella, was published in 2015. She holds an MFA in Creative Writing from West Virginia Wesleyan College.

Jeff Hardin is the author of *Fall Sanctuary,* recipient of the Nicholas Roerich Prize, and *Notes for a Praise Book,* selected by Toi Derricotte for the Jacar Press Book Award, as well as *Restoring the Narrative* and *Small Revolution*. His poems have been published in *The New Republic, The Southern Review, The Gettysburg Review, Hotel Amerika, Southern Poetry Review,* and elsewhere. He teaches at Columbia State Community College in Columbia, Tennessee.

Chris Holbrook, a native of Knott County, Kentucky, is the author of the short story collections *Upheaval* and *Hell and Ohio: Stories of Southern Appalachia,* which received the Thomas and Lillie D. Chaffin Award for Appalachian Writing. A graduate of the Iowa Writers' Workshop, Holbrook is associate professor of English at Morehead State University.

Eric Janken's poetry has been in *Southern Cultures, Regarding Arts & Letters,* and *Aethlon: Journal of Sport Literature,* and his interviews and reviews have appeared in *Carolina Quarterly.* He is a graduate of Appalachian State University.

Emily Masters is a senior English major at Berea College where she works as a teaching assistant for Silas House and as a student editor for *Appalachian Heritage* and *Apollon* e-journal. She is from Monteagle, Tennessee, where she lives on a farm with her family. Her work has recently been published in *The Pikeville Review.*

Jane Miller's poetry has appeared in the *Iron Horse Literary Review, Summerset Review, cahoodaloodaling, Mojave River Review,* and *Pittsburgh Poetry Review,* among others. A nominee for Best New Poets and Best of the Net, she was a finalist in the 2017 Red Wheelbarrow Poetry Contest.

Josh Ness is founder of Nashville Explorers Club, a collective of avid creatives who are proud to have grown up in Nashville and keen to show off what the Nashville life looks like. Visit the club's website at www.nashvilleexplorers.club.

David Salner lived in West Virginia and has worked as a cab driver, power plant laborer, and machinist. His writing has appeared in *Threepenny Review, Iowa Review, Prairie Schooner, Salmagundi, River Styx, Beloit Poetry Journal,* and many other magazines. His third book is *Blue Morning Light* and features poems on the paintings of American artist George Bellows.

Savannah Sipple is the author of *WWJD & Other Poems* (Sibling Rivalry Press, 2019). A writer from east Kentucky, her poems have recently been published in *Appalachian Heritage, Talking River, The Offing,* and *The Louisville Review.* She is also the recipient of grants from the Money for Women/Barbara Deming Memorial Fund and the Kentucky Foundation for Women.

Kelsey A. Solomon teaches writing and literature at Walters State Community College as an Instructor of English. Her most recent publications in poetry can be found in *Pine Mountain Sand & Gravel: Appalachia Under 30* and the *Anthology of Appalachian Writers.*

Nicole Stockburger is an MFA in Creative Writing candidate at the University of North Carolina at Greensboro. She splits her time between Greensboro and Mount Airy where she helps her partner market-farm an acre of organic vegetables. Her poems are forthcoming from *Comestible* and other journals.

Susan O'Dell Underwood directs the creative writing program at Carson-Newman University. The author of two chapbooks, her work has appeared in *Oxford American, Rock & Sling, Crab Orchard Review, Bellevue Literary Review,* and *The Southern Poetry Anthology: Tennessee.* Her first full-length book of poems, *The Book Of Awe,* is forthcoming from Iris Press.

Mary Jane White holds an MFA from the Iowa Writers' Workshop and has received NEA Fellowships in poetry and translation. Her first book, *Starry Sky to Starry Sky,* was published in 1988, and her work has appeared in *AGNI* (online), *The American Poetry Review, The Iowa Review, Crazyhorse, The Anthology of Magazine Verse and Yearbook of American Poetry, The Black Warrior Review, The Louisville Review,* and in other publications.

Lois Wolfe is a West Virginia native who now lives in Florida, where she has led the Marathon Writers Workshop since 2015. She is the author of two novels, *The Schemers* (Bantam, 1991) and *Mask of Night* (Doubleday/Bantam, 1993), and numerous pieces of short fiction, poetry, essays and book reviews.